Praise for *Visiting Hours*

"This gripping memoir is every bit as chilling as the darkest Gillian Flynn novel—except this nonfiction account is based entirely on real events. . . . It's emotional, powerful, and, oddly enough, beautiful."　　　　　—Lynsey Eidell, *Glamour*

"Enthralling, thought provoking, and deeply empathic, *Visiting Hours* explores how loss and trauma affects everyone in its periphery."　　　　　—*Biographile*

"A haunting meditation on human fragility."
　　　　　—Rachel Martin, NPR

"A gripping and poignant memoir."　　　　　—*Kirkus Reviews*

"Riveting and visceral."
　　　　　—Mardi Jo Link, *Star Tribune* (Minneapolis)

"I couldn't put down this April release, *Visiting Hours: A Memoir of Friendship and Murder*, by Amy Butcher. Their senior year at Gettysburg College in Pennsylvania, Amy's good friend Kevin walks her home, returns to his apartment, and stabs to death his ex-girlfriend. How such a dastardly act affects their friendship—or how it might affect any friendship of our own—kept me riveted."
　　　　　—Dannye Romine Powell, *The Charlotte Observer*

D0064237

"There are horrors in *Visiting Hours*—some of them emotional, some incomprehensibly not. But what rises above it all in this exhilaratingly honest and brutal debut is what might be the book's most disturbingly beautiful element: its tribute to memory, its testament of love, and its wide-eyed inquiry into just how long those two things really last."

—John D'Agata, author of *About a Mountain*

"Amy Butcher asks the two hardest questions: what do we mean to ourselves and what do we mean to each other? She asks in innocence and responds with hard-earned experience and wisdom to share. You will need to give *Visiting Hours* away and buy another for yourself so you have someone to talk to about it. You will keep an eye out for this writer and what she will do next. It is not right that she is so smart, so talented, and so young all at the same time. Yes, hers is a debut to envy and here we are at the very beginning."

—Robert Olmstead, author of *Coal Black Horse*

"*Visiting Hours* is the culmination of Amy Butcher's many talents: beautifully dense yet accessible prose rendered with complete honesty. She will make you question everyone you've ever thought you've known."

—Mary Miller, author of *The Last Days of California*

"Amy Butcher has written an incredible portrait of trauma. In crisp, beautiful pose, Butcher revisits an extraordinary and terrible night that will come to haunt and trouble her forever. What is the nature of traumatic memory? Whose sadness do we have claim to? What can be done when people we love do terrible things? Butcher's generous and honest meditation on how traumatic memory can shape ordinary lives will make you a better and more empathetic person."

—Jen Percy, author of *Demon Camp*

"*Visiting Hours* is a mystery of the highest order, not merely a whodunit, as we know from the outset who killed whom, but a mystery of the human heart, exploring the ambiguous motivations of an otherwise gentle man who became a murderer and a young woman who couldn't stop being his friend. A page-turner for its pathos and gorgeous attention to language, a coming-of-age story like no other, Amy Butcher has written a story of no easy answers and unparalleled sensitivity."

—Robin Hemley, author of *Do-Over!*

VISITING
HOURS

VISITING HOURS

A Memoir of
Friendship
and Murder

AMY BUTCHER

Blue Rider Press
New York

blue
rider
press

An imprint of Penguin Random House LLC
375 Hudson Street
New York, New York 10014

Copyright © 2015 by Amy Butcher

Parts of this book have appeared in slightly altered form in *The Colorado Review, Guernica, The Iowa Review, The Rumpus, Salon, Upstreet,* and *Vela.*

BLUE RIDER PRESS IS A REGISTERED TRADEMARK AND ITS COLOPHON IS A
TRADEMARK OF PENGUIN RANDOM HOUSE LLC

THE LIBRARY OF CONGRESS HAS CATALOGUED THE HARDCOVER EDITION AS FOLLOWS:

Butcher, Amy, date.
Visiting hours : a memoir of friendship and murder / Amy Butcher.
p.   cm.
Includes bibliographical references.
ISBN 978-0-399-17207-6
1. Schaeffer, Kevin.   2. Butcher, Amy, date.   3. Murderers—Pennsylvania—
Biography.   4. Murder—Pennsylvania.   5. Friendship.   I. Title.
HV6248.S3817B87   2015   2014040712
364.152'3092—dc23

Blue Rider Press hardcover edition: April 2015
Blue Rider Press trade paperback edition: April 2016
Blue Rider Press trade paperback ISBN: 978-0-399-18339-3

Printed in the United States of America
1   3   5   7   9   10   8   6   4   2

Book design by Michelle McMillian

for my parents,
and for theirs

There is so little to remember of anyone—an anecdote, a conversation at table. But every memory is turned over and over again, every word, however chance, written in the heart in the hope that memory will fulfill itself, and become flesh, and that the wanderers will find a way home, and the perished, whose lack we always feel, will step through the door finally and stroke our hair with dreaming, habitual fondness, not having meant to keep us waiting long.

—MARILYNNE ROBINSON

Author's Note

This is a work of creative nonfiction. It is based on the factual record of Kevin Schaeffer's crime and my own memory of our friendship and the events described herein, as well as the opinions of and stories told to me by the people I am most inclined to believe. Certain details, including the names and identifying characteristics of certain individuals, have been altered for the sake of privacy.

A portion of all proceeds from this book has been split evenly between the Stop Dating Violence project, sponsored by the EMILY Fund, and the National Alliance on Mental Illness.

VISITING
HOURS

Prologue

In April of 2009, in the early hours of morning, my friend
Kevin walked me home from a neighborhood bar a block
away. Our trip took us past a convenience store and a pet shop
that sold canine tuxes and wedding dresses, made-to-order
dog biscuits, and raincoats and plastic booties. We stood before
the storefront and I pointed to their display—*Do you see those
tiny laces? Can you imagine that yellow raincoat?*—and Kevin
laughed, nudging me along.

"It's late," he said. "Let's go."

Kevin was acting calm that night, collected, *normal*, although I'd later wish he hadn't been. *He was acting so strangely*,
I'd want to be able to say, because at least that would make
some sense. But the Kevin that walked me home that night
was the same one I'd always known. We reached the stairs that
led to my apartment, and we hugged goodnight, and I closed
the door, and then Kevin turned for home—*for bed*, I thought,
for television. Upstairs in my narrow, dark apartment, I brushed

my teeth and climbed into bed, and in the morning, I woke early to watch *The Price Is Right* in my pajamas.

I didn't know then what had happened—that two hours after seeing me home, Kevin experienced what doctors would later call a "psychotic break," or a state of "psychotic dissociation," or they would say, very simply, "He was not aware of his environment." But all that really meant was that, whatever his awareness of right or wrong, Kevin could not act upon that notion as he stabbed to death his former girlfriend. He struck Emily Silverstein twenty-seven times in the neck and upper torso, then asked a friend to phone the police, saying he was so sorry, and would they come?

He said, "I'll be waiting for you outside."

The police lowered him into their squad car just an hour before I awoke, and in a statement an hour later, he'd say, "I completely lost control."

In my quiet, bright apartment, I watched the colorful wheel spin and spin, the cameras panning over Jet Skis, entertainment systems, and dining sets. One woman won a car, and she jumped up and down, clutching her heart.

1

FROM THE FIFTH-FLOOR WINDOW of the Comfort Suites in
Edinboro, Pennsylvania, the State Correctional Institution at
Albion is nothing more than a nondescript, yellow haze—a
fog that curls in the predawn darkness like liquid and settles
lightly along the mountains. It is dim, so dim it could be mis-
taken for a factory, or the parking lot of a grocery store, or
some sleepy ski resort where men spread snow across a distant
mountain. But of course I know it's not. Of course I know
exactly what those lights mean: men in watchtowers, roving
beams, barbwire so thick and sharp I imagine sea monsters
with glinting teeth.

From my place high above them, behind the glass, I can
feel the outside air push in, cold against the gauzy window. It
is late November, the month I've long considered to be the
loneliest of the year, a time when even the landscape itself
turns gray and gnarled with what is yet to come. But in the
darkness, there are no trees, no yellowing fields, no twisted

roots. In the darkness, there is only darkness, and it stretches out and into the mountains, interrupted only infrequently by the lights of well-lit living rooms and front porch spotlights. They blink between tree branches, and within them, I imagine women setting down casseroles on green linen tablecloths, children racing from darkened dens, family dogs curled beside brick fireplaces as logs first crackle and then begin to burn. I imagine them as if I know them because their peace was once my own, their quiet once my quiet, and because their imagined evenings are far preferable to the reality that is this dawn: how in a moment, day will break, and I've awakened before it happens so that I might first stand and look toward this dark horizon—toward Kevin out there, too, of course—before the sunrise rushes in.

There's nothing to be scared of, I think, and from a distance, that much is true. From a distance, his prison is merely a light: a haze so small and unobtrusive I can hide it by simply lifting my thumb. I raise my finger to the darkened glass and move it in and out of my line of vision. I see first a prison, and then no prison, prison again and then just my thumb.

Now you see it, I think, *now you don't*, and while I wish I could stand at this window forever—*How much nicer*, I think, *just looking*—I've already come this far, so instead, I pull and secure the blinds in the same way that I now do everything—a little slower than I should—then take my bag from the bedside table and make my way to the darkened bathroom.

What you need is a long, hot shower, I think, and for a moment, this does the trick. I stand beneath the pulsing water and look at how clean and white the tub, how warm and wet the air, the mist filming the bathroom mirror in swipes from the maid's Windexing the day before.

This is fine, I think. *You're fine.*

But back on the cold, white tiles, I realize I've forgotten about my neckline. It's the little things—now and always—that throw me most off guard: a spot on my tomato, the way a man says my name. Anyone else would just cut around it, or think a name is just a name. But after that night, the small things are everything: proof of what cannot be controlled. A bad spot— in men or vegetables—is a thing I will not risk. I throw the tomato in the compost and obsess about the man.

"Didn't he sound *creepy* when he said my name?" I've asked on more than one occasion. "There is *no way* I'm dating him."

Friends joke that I am crazy and admit this to me out loud.

"He seemed nice enough to me," they say. "Don't you think you're overreacting?"

But no, of course I don't, because I was the last person Kevin saw that night—the last woman before Emily. He walked me home and then he killed her. He wanted to "make sure [I] got in safe." And what it means now—nearly three years later—is that I still find traces of that evening on everything: in the way I slice my vegetables, in the way I do not date. I walk my dog beside a reservoir, and even then, I think of him.

It's like momentum, I want to say, and what I mean is how it looks when a rock strikes a body of water—how ripples can form and move even long after the stone has sunk.

. . .

The problem, as I see it, is that I can only anticipate so much—prepare myself for the fourteen-hour journey, pack foil-wrapped sandwiches and ginger ales—but still I know that no amount of preparation can help me envision our reunion. It's for this very reason, in fact, I've spent the past few weeks in a state of panic; I've barely eaten and have not slept. And yet I've considered everything I could think to think and planned my trip accordingly.

Something so small I haven't thought of—well, that's what's most disarming. It throws everything off balance.

This neckline, for example.

It is small and shallow, a beige waffle-print crewneck, a shirt I've worn to brunches and picnics, Longwood Gardens and a choral concert, and it was for these reasons I chose it two days ago when I packed; I thought those good memories could mean something. I pictured them germlike and small, little filaments of contentment and good nature that could last the whole day through: as guards ran their hands along my torso, as they waved magnetic wands over my arms and legs. "Right this way, ma'am," they'd tell me coolly, but in my mind I'd be wearing my picnic blanket, a purple orchid, a day spent by a calm Midwestern lake. An entire history of memorable moments, right there across my frame. And wouldn't I be grateful? That because I'd thought it through I was in this shirt and not another?

And yet never in my careful planning did I think to consider my shirt's neckline, which—modest as it is—fails to conceal the thick black straps of the sports bra I'm wearing underneath it.

They line my neck like a harness, and if I want to ensure my visitation, I know they cannot show under any circumstance. *Failure to comply with dress code guidelines*, I'd read, *will result in prohibition.*

It would take no more than one irritable guard—one woman with a pen and clipboard—to notice my bra's cotton straps and then remove me from her prison lobby. "Indecent," she would say, or maybe she'd say nothing to me at all but would still force me to vacate her property; I would not see Kevin and he would not see me. And if I'd be grateful for that denial—well, it's difficult now to say.

Of all the things to worry about, I never anticipated clothing. Soon there would be cameras and guns and guards. There would be Tasers, probably. There would almost certainly be dogs.

And while I knew it wouldn't be easy, I thought at least I was prepared. Hundreds of people had already gone to great lengths—in Internet forums, on official government websites—to articulate the experience for me, to help me envision it before I even arrived in Albion. These were people who adopted Internet pseudonyms, usernames, created accounts by typing in the name of their third-grade teacher, or the town where they were born—Yankeesgrrl, they named themselves, LovnMyDominican—and as Guest, I took their information: printing from their websites, organizing their paragraphs, bullet-pointing their experiential tips. I looked at all the websites: JailGuide.com, Offenders' Families Helpline, Conversant Life, even *Psychology Today*.

"Visiting Prison Can Make You an Emotional Basket Case," read one headline I clicked and skimmed.

I printed everything—just in case—and then arranged the files in a manila folder in descending order of authenticity: first the guidelines for Pennsylvania penitentiary visits, then the letter from Kevin's mother with additional personal advice, and finally a detailed list of what seemed the most pressing dress code procedures. I wrote in every margin. I highlighted what seemed important. *This happens at Kevin's prison, too, I think*, I wrote, and, *Maybe look into this further?*

Because I've done the research, I know I must wear sneakers. Open-toed shoes—and leggings, for that matter—are recent additions to the list of banned apparel. *But the metal ends on the tips of laces*, one user wrote in a forum on visitation, *can set off the alarms*, so I pull on a pair of white Ked slip-ons and think, *I look like I belong on a boat.*

Drinking fancy cocktails from salt-rimmed glasses, I think. *Eating cheese from tiny pucks.*

But because it's a prison I'm about to enter—not the ramp to someone's yacht—I refrain from barrettes and bracelets, metal-banded hair ties, bobby pins. The dress code states there can be no hair clips or even earrings. There can be absolutely no fake gold rings.

I hadn't thought about it when I packed; I thought a ring could come in handy. Sometimes I find I wear one now just because: in new cities, at cocktail parties. I slip it on my left hand and pretend it signifies some sort of love, but of course it signifies fear; Kevin has made me wary of strange, new men.

It's crazy, I think at times: how a ring from a dollar store does the work I haven't found a way yet to do with language.

"It's complicated," I'd have to say. "I want to get to know you, but *I'm afraid*."

"My friend walked me home and then murdered his girl-friend," I'd say. "So you seem sweet and all, but some other time."

The ring does this work for me. I don't have to feel pressure to engage a man. I don't have to feign interest and then disinterest.

I'm just a woman wearing a ring.

But of course in prison that's not allowed, so I slip the gold band from my finger and place it on the bathroom counter, beside the soap and my travel toothbrush, a one-ounce lotion that smells of sea, and while I know enough now to feel ready, still I know that I know nothing, really.

That I have never been inside a prison—much less a maximum-security facility—was never a problem for me before.

"But *everyone's* been to a prison," a friend's boyfriend told me recently. "What you're doing is nothing new."

He'd said it like it was a point of pride—sitting there, his feet kicked up on a fraying armrest, even his body language suggesting superiority. His implication was that he was better—in a real and tangible way—for having this experience. He thought it was fodder with which to mock me.

"You talk about it like it's unique," he said. "But everyone I *know* has been to a prison."

"Sure," I said, "I know that," but in truth, I didn't, really. Later, I asked our friend, saying, "Have *you* ever been in a prison?"

"I visited my brother once," she said, "but he was always in and out. Small misdemeanors, usually—nothing like what you're doing."

What you're doing. I wish I knew. At times, I tell myself it can be simple: I am just visiting a friend from college. We are reuniting, *catching up*, in what is just one of many reunions I've done since graduation. *It's not terribly unlike lunch in Baltimore*, I think, *or meeting for coffee in Washington, D.C.*

Except, of course, it's prison.

And because I've never been in one, I have no idea what to expect. I mean beyond the letters that Kevin sends, the things I've researched independently. I have absolutely no idea what it's like to walk through metal detectors and a row of guards just to see someone you love. Not *love* as in romantic, but *One night I cut his hair on a porch bathed in yellow light.*

Or, *We completed three days of a ten-day juice fast, but called it off for vanilla soft-serve.*

Or, *He was a classmate and then a friend and then a maximum-security inmate.*

I didn't know, then, until I read it online, that the underwire in a traditional bra is enough to fail a maximum-security prison's high-sensitivity metal detectors. *I had to pierce the fabric with my keys and squeeze the underwire out in a bathroom stall,* one woman wrote, *and it ruined my best bra, not to mention no support.*

But even without the wire, there was the issue of straps: they should be thin, I learned, and shouldn't show, and they should be any color but pink. My sports bra is black, one of three from a Kmart discount pack, and it's as simple as Lycra can be—a shade meant not to show sweat, a fit that is both modest and neutral—but already I'm in violation of the prison's strict dress code, because there are my straps, and my shirt doesn't hide them.

Jesus, I think, as if I can will them to disappear.

From my suitcase beneath the counter, I search for another top, but they are all V-necked, slim, tight, or feminine—shirts adorned with sequins or stripes, lace, colors, and fabrics meant to flatter the female figure. These are not shirts for prison. These are shirts for a magazine ad: a girl walking down a sidewalk, a girl eating an ice-cream cone with sprinkles. She's holding a yellow umbrella, maybe, a white pug on a pink leash beside her, and for a second I allow the thought: *I wish I could be her, instead.*

I'd name the dog Kit-Kat or Pancake, I think, *and never think about prison again.*

Instead I pull a safety pin from the side compartment and pull, *stretch*, pinch the fabric together behind my neck and fasten the pin above my spine so the straps are secure behind my neck, low and out of view. *There*, I think, triumphant—there is nothing visible but shirt and skin. But the moment passes once I remember the metal detectors. How of course this just makes things worse.

This visit is one I've spent over two years planning, and yet had I really been prepared, I would've tried this outfit on sooner.

A test run, if you will.

Had I known to anticipate this particular problem, I might've even considered buying a prison-friendly bra online, an item I learned about only recently while browsing PrisonTalk.com.

That's how I always gain his attention, one inmate's wife wrote in a forum on visitations. *I own a pink one with a lacy trim.* And as if to further what seemed obvious, she'd placed a winking emoticon beside her text.

There's no way that those exist, I'd thought, running a search in Google for confirmation, but sure enough, they appeared: online-only vendors who sell prison-appropriate intimates not only to correctional facility inmates, but to the average at-home consumer. I browsed them—because why not?—and was impressed by their selection: the variety of fabrics, cuts, and shades, and how all of them were wire-free, encouraging a more natural visitation experience. American Detention Supplies, for example, sells an underwireless, blush "Glamorise Magic Lift" bra, and there's also the Cross Your Heart–style cream bra, though it's only available in bulk.

There is a certain kind of strangeness, however, in ordering a prison bra online. Kevin is not my lover, not my boyfriend; he never was and never will be. Kevin is just a friend, a man I might otherwise fear, but he is my friend, first and foremost, and should not require special undergarments.

So the sports bra will be fine, I think.

The sports bra has to be.

. . .

Everything felt easier before this moment. Last night, in the parking lot of the Comfort Suites, I'd bent across my bumper in the yellowing light of evening, the yellowing light of fall, and it seemed simpler even then.

I thought I could predict what might occur.

I was surveying my trunk ahead of time for items that might otherwise seem suspicious—ropes, nails, a hammer, netting—and I was calm, despite it all. I thought, *This is absolutely no problem. Look how fine you feel!*

My fear was that I'd panic. That I'd arrive in Albion and see Kevin's prison and think simply, *No.* That afternoon, as I got off the highway, I'd even considered driving past it— turning right at the only traffic light instead of going straight. *What's one little detour,* I'd thought, *especially if it makes the morning drive go smoother?* I'd know exactly where I was going, feel familiar with the trip. But I didn't trust myself to do it: see his prison and then, later, return.

Instead I went to the hotel, checked in, bought a soda. In the near-empty parking lot, I put my key in the still-warm ignition and then leaned down into my car, combing through the contents of a box my father once insisted stay in my trunk. *Your emergency supply kit,* he called it, and it was nothing more than an empty wine box—MONDAVI, it read in black—but he'd filled it with a Red Cross kit, an army blanket, two jumper cables, a set of flares. There was an ice scraper in there, a bottle of Windex, a roll of toilet paper, a beat-up baseball.

"Just in case you ever break down," he'd said. "I'll feel better knowing you have this much."

There was a pocketknife. There was duct tape.

I turned the items over as the parking lot lights clicked on. A few yards away, a man called to his wife as she crossed the grassy median that separated our hotel from a convenience store.

"A Snickers bar," he said, "maybe get some Tastykakes?"

Bring a roll of quarters from a bank, please, Kevin wrote me in his last letter. *That way we can get snacks from the vending machines!*

There were microwavable pizzas in there, he told me. There were Doritos. There were Cheesey Puffs.

I fast before each visit, he wrote. *I haven't had those things in years!*

Of course I'd brought the quarters—they were already tightly packed in their required see-through change purse in the passenger seat beside my road map. I'd picked them up at the bank a few days earlier, standing in line for what felt like forever, but never in my careful planning did I think to get toll money for myself, and I'd been tempted on the highway to split that roll open, take a quarter or two, but I knew that if it was ripped, I could not bring it inside the prison, because of *drugs*, a user wrote. Powder could be taped between the coins, I'd learned, and so, too, could razor blades.

That's crazy, I'd thought, incredulous, and yet I valued Kevin enough not to test it. Instead, I got off the highway and went through a drive-thru ATM, and when the machine spit out my cash in twenties, I cursed and slammed the wheel, then drove to the small off-ramp McDonald's to beg a cashier for smaller bills.

"I'm so sorry," I said, embarrassed, "but mostly I need quarters and fives and ones."

The emergency kit was like that, too. It was amazing, in retrospect, how for nearly ten years I'd kept that crappy wine box inside my trunk, listened to it rattle with every turn I made, every pothole I hit, and even on the rare Saturdays when I thought to clean my car—slipping quarters into a cylindrical machine beside an automatic car wash—I always first turned the box back upright, refilled its contents that had spilled across the trunk, and moved the vacuum hose around and under it, thinking, *Do I really need these things?*

A tarp? A bunch of zip ties?

I'd spent that day, in fact, listening to them roll around as I drove from my home in Iowa back to this state I had left three years ago. I passed dairy farms, standing cattle, trailer parks, and flocks of geese, and every ten or twenty miles, I'd hear *clunk*. I'd hear *clunk clunk*.

The first aid kit slamming into the backseat.

The box tipping over despite the blanket.

And while he'd hoped they'd keep me safe, my father had no way of predicting what these items might mean to a prison guard, which I'd soon find out. I'd pull into the parking lot of the State Correctional Institution at Albion, pick a spot, and pop my trunk. My 2001 Toyota Camry would be susceptible to a warden-issued search, and I knew this because of Kevin's mother, who warned me in her letter.

The second time we went, she wrote, *they came out to search the car, and that was really weird.*

The guards would pat me down, maybe. Search my glove

compartment. They would look underneath my seats or in my console or under mats. I could not show up with my gift store pocketknife, my roll of near-vintage duct tape. The flares, too, were suspicious, as was the box of matches.

Even the jumper cables had sharp edges.

Get rid of everything you question, she wrote, *or they might not let you in.*

Fine by me, I thought, pulling the box across the pavement until the cardboard frayed and bent. I propped it against the dumpster and wiped my hands against my jeans, but when I turned around to see it—beside an empty Coke can, beside a hot-pink, broken stroller—I only saw my father.

I could not leave it there.

This is ludicrous, I thought, picking the box back up from the bottom, careful to support the now thinning cardboard. I carried it that way across the parking lot and through the hotel lobby, into the elevator, up five floors, and when finally I reached my room—with its microwavable cookies and whirlpool bathtub, the note that reads *We Care!*—I set it down beside my suitcase and my preplanned visitation clothes, then drew the hotel blinds to obscure the glow emanating from what I trust is Kevin's home.

This is not where I expected to be, three years out from that April evening. I often thought that by this point, I'd be able to look at what Kevin had done as if I were standing on a distant shoreline, staring out at an even more distant pinpoint—an event I could identify as pivotal in my development that I had experienced and then moved on from. Above all, it seemed this: The past, of course, would pass.

Instead, it remains large and looming; I find I think of Kevin all the time. Occasionally when I am happy, and nearly every time I'm not. He is the face that triggers everything: the many things I love and fear. Because of what he did, I feel grateful to be alive. To pick and eat a raspberry. To draw back the blinds to summer sun.

But because of what Kevin did, it's fear I feel when that sun goes down.

It's complicated, to put it simply: how this person who remains my friend I love and fear in equal measure. I want to say this is not the case—*You were not the one affected*, I often think—but because I still don't understand what happened, I send him a letter every month. I put money in his prison account, and order books for him off Amazon, and print him pictures, and print my life.

Here's what I've been up to, I write, because I know it's what Kevin longs for most: not his freedom, necessarily, but to know a life not stuck in stagnation. He seeks a break from the mundane, a way to feel inspired, a letter that says *I miss you*, and *I remember*, and *I care*.

Do you remember the good times? he asked once, and yes, of course I do.

And there were years like that, I remind myself, *four whole years before this happened.*

And yet I find I think of Kevin now and I only ever think of *this* place, *this* smell, *this* lighting. His world, so clean and chemical. I think of jumpsuits and facial hair, mounted cameras, guns, and guards. I think about his reading glasses—how those first three weeks of his incarceration, he begged for but could not have them.

Because of the glass, he later wrote. He could break the metal frames, his mother explained. Flick the sharp edge across his wrists.

So even now, all these years later, I find it hard while enjoying *anything* not to think of my parallel: a man my same age and height who—because of those few dark hours—will now spend the majority of his life in a maximum-security prison. For all the freedom that is mine to enjoy, I'm unwillingly tethered to that trauma; often, when in transit, I find I take a seat beside a stranger and find myself navigating to the subject, to this story that is not mine.

"I think that minds can break," I say, crossing my legs or adjusting the overhead light.

I like, I think, the ambiguity and temporal nature that traveling, especially, provides: how here we are together, two strangers sharing an oval window, a foot and a half of legroom, and two hours or so of time. On a plane, on a train, on a bus, I can say the things I want, covet the full attention of an absolute stranger. So I tell whoever is there beside me that mental illness is an epidemic, that so, too, is incarceration, that the men and women who remain in our nation's jails represent one-fourth of all the people currently incarcerated on earth.

"We have more incarcerated people than in Rwanda," I say. "More than Russia, even."

Nearly two and a half million Americans live their days

within a prison, looping barbwire spirals their sharp perimeter, and more daunting than those spaces is that the rate of mental illness within those confines is five times that of the general population. And since 2001, that rate rises steadily with every year.

"It's a misconception," I tell anyone—the stranger unfurling a Delta napkin, the woman dog-earing the pages of her SkyMall catalogue—"that crime is on the rise; in fact, instances of criminal activity have dropped over a quarter these past forty years, and yet the rate of incarceration has quadrupled."

And what am I, they want to know. A doctor, some sort of clinician? A researcher? Scientist?

"I just care about these issues," I say, though I do not tell them why.

That reason *why*, of course, is why I'm standing in this hotel's bathroom. Why I'm heaving at my bra straps, tugging, pinching the fabric into place. I hold court over these conversations, imagining I've imparted a stranger with some newfound wisdom, but in reality I'm just a fellow passenger—the stranger in 22A—who will soon deplane and remove her luggage and traverse a narrow jet bridge. Who will hail a taxi, who will disappear. And what effect—if any—I've had, there's no real way for me to know.

With my final moments in the hotel bathroom, I try to make things fun. *Head, shoulders, knees, and toes*, I think, scanning my body for metal buttons. I run my fingers first over pant legs and then my torso and then my neck.

I find I often pretend it's a game—having a friend in a place like his. Some mornings, I walk to my mailbox and attempt to predict what's waiting there: a list of the books Kevin's read most recently, a request for photos of a Matisse painting.

Send me The School of Athens *by Raphael*, he writes. *Send me* The Red Vineyard, *or* The Sower, *or* Prisoners Exercising *by Vincent van Gogh.*

Sometimes, Kevin just wants a picture—of me, of my apartment in Iowa, of anyone.

Send me some from college, he says. *I'm beginning to forget your faces.*

I oblige him every time. I head down to the public library, type in my username, print in color. Or I look up French kings on Wikipedia and print all twelve pages, including citations. I stand beside the librarian's desk and say, "The printer's out of ink." I say, "The printer's out of paper."

I pay fifty cents a page, but there's no way for me to know the things a man in prison needs. *If I were in prison*, I think, *I hope someone would do this for me.* Because what if I wanted to learn a new language? What if I still wanted to feel moved by art? If the point of prison is to be kept from society, must society remain kept from a prison?

The women in the library—they are decades older and call me hon. They stand beside the machines, pulling paper from its careful packaging. They press START. They press RESUME.

"I'm not entirely certain how this works," they say, and I say, "It's no problem. I have all day."

These women think I'm doing research, maybe, or they think I'm curious, an avid learner. They think I'm an art history major, that I'm completing a paper on Pablo Picasso. *I think he was a real fine artist*, I'll write, *and undoubtedly, he made a big impact.*

In no way do I think these women suspect these pages are for a murderer.

"Thanks," I say when they've finished, and then I scoop the files into a manila envelope I'll later mail on my walk home.

But the games—they make this fun. They are the only things that do. They suppress the grinding panic, the feeling of a child sitting Indian-style across my chest. This is how I refer to it now—the seizing anxiety I feel when I think of Kevin. I joke to friends and family because it's the only way I know to cope.

I say, "Today the child is patient." I say, "Today, there's a temper tantrum."

Some days, it feels like a million tiny feet grinding deep into my esophagus; everything seizes up and it becomes diffi-cult, even, to breathe. So *head, shoulders, knees, and toes*, I think, and then an alteration: *feet and tummy, arms and chin.*

And while I can prepare this morning for as long as I'd like—sing any song I want—more than guards, or drugs, or dogs, it's my face I worry about.

My face gives me away.

In the weeks before this visit, I've become a distant version of myself—blemishes appeared beneath my lips and my eyes puffed around their rims. They're subtle parts of a bigger whole, surface-level discrepancies, things Kevin may not even notice. *But this is not my face*, I think, pushing my fingers into my cheeks. *This is not my face at all.*

This is the face, instead, of a woman who knows she'll soon be sitting in a room with murderers, with rapists, with men who have killed strangers. With men who have killed children. And it doesn't matter that Kevin's my friend—he killed a woman once, and I have the tired, pale features that prove it, right there, across my face. They concede that I've never been to a prison, even if everyone else in the world somehow has, and there's nothing I want more now than the ability to hide them. So I apply concealer and a little blush, but forgo lipstick, mascara, eyeliner. The goal is not to look attractive for Kevin; it is only to look right, *normal*, the way I looked for four years when Kevin glanced across the classroom at me, or sat beside me in the cafeteria, or smiled at me in the bar just four hours before his arrest.

I want to be the person that he remembers and not the person I've since become.

I owe that much to him, I think, no longer certain even I believe it.

2

FROM THE HOTEL, it's a twenty-five-minute drive west to Albion, and I spend the time watching the landscape as it unravels: first houses and then no houses, gravel drives and then flat land. This is rural Pennsylvania, a place just like the towns Kevin and I both come from, a place so similar to where we were raised that I watch for signs for shoofly pie.

And perhaps it should be easy, in this end, to first consider our beginning, but the problem with my memory is that it functions now against him. In the three years since Kevin's arrest, I find myself forgetting the simplest things: the way he sounded when laughing, the snack he most enjoyed. A scientist friend told me recently that this phenomenon is not uncommon—that in an attempt to forget material it finds particularly upsetting, the mind begins to lose things, and that loss is more or less on purpose.

"It's not a conscious effort," he said. "You have to think

about it like wiping a whiteboard. The smudge still remains, of course, but for the most part, the text is gone."

I prefer to imagine my brain as an insubordinate teenager: bumbling, anxious, and acne-pocked, nervous but charismatic. My brain is charming, in its own way, in how it can't seem to keep things straight: *Where are your keys? Where's your homework? Why are you home so late? What's your problem?*

Why are you always forgetting the things that should matter most?

What should matter most is the pre-prison Kevin, and at times, I try to remember him. I sit at a traffic light and imagine my friend eating a slice of pizza, look at the toppings, try to recall which he likes best. Or I imagine him kicking a cigarette butt from our porch to the pavement, watch it shoot out from his red-sneakered foot. The floorboards beneath us are cornflower blue, and they're splintered, and buckled in places, and while it's been five years since we lived there last, I can picture them better now than I can Kevin.

It was a lovely porch, I find myself thinking.

These memories are things I should have: Kevin eating cookies from a styrofoam plate, the way he said "water" or "creek." I crave what is otherwise ordinary—a foundation for how normal he was. And while I know this, I can't remember, because they antagonize who he has become and who I must understand him, at all times, to be: a maximum-security inmate who spends his days inside a jail cell, reading books and the *New York Times*; a man who, regardless of anything else, stabbed a nineteen-year-old girl to death.

But the problem with my memory—it's not because Kevin and I weren't close. It's that I've put so much energy into being his friend that I've forgotten what isn't important. I've forgotten who he used to be.

Those memories are completely gone, a whiteboard that time's wiped clean.

What I've held on to these past three years, instead, is just a handful of vague abstractions: a moment here, a moment there. His fork moving across the table, upright, wobbling like a person. It's rocking from side to side, personified whimsically, and then he spears it into my pizza, pulling a pepperoni from the slice on my plate.

"Hey," I say, "that's mine," and he says, "Not anymore, *it'sinmymouth!*"

And perhaps it should be troubling—oftentimes, I think it is—that I have not forgotten what Kevin did; nor have I forgotten how that day felt. I remember even sensual details: the coolness of my parents' dark living room, the pine-scented candle by the sink in the bathroom. All these specifics that exist on the periphery of the moment I saw my friend's face on the nine o'clock news.

But if asked—beyond them—to count my memories of Kevin from before his incarceration, I would, admittedly, flounder. Those memories are ghosts: once present but now lacking shape, lacking specificity, lacking a sense of conviction. And yet I remain unbothered by my brain's selectiveness; I think I understand why it does what it does. It seems necessary, in ways, that I forget all that complicates Kevin. What good is it to remember how considerate he was? How courteous, how kind? It is stressful to recall those attributes in conjunction with the violence they caused, regardless.

These skips in my memory, I'm told, are installed for my own protection; it's too much, in other words, for a mind to hold on to such oppositions. Kevin once filled many mental spaces simply by chewing a piece of gum, or bobbing his head to a Snoop Dogg track, filling a cup with orange soda or whistling idly as he walked. But now he fills those spaces with images of tubs and brains and bars; I think of Kevin and I think, *Inmate.* I find when I think of him, I think, *He's sick.*

What's problematic, then, is not my memory, but Kevin's own expectation—that because I was there, I remember it all.

Your visit will be an exhilarating blur! he wrote in his most recent letter. *It probably sounds cliché on paper, but you're going to give me a glimpse of my old life, cheerful reminiscences, even laughter! I haven't laughed since coming here, if you can believe it,* he wrote, and of course—of course—I could.

But seeing you will be amazing, he wrote. *Exactly like old times. You remember me for who I was, not who I've become these past three years.*

I know, I wrote in response. *I remember everything, and I can't wait.*

What is unequivocally true: Kevin and I met on our third day at Gettysburg College, so early into freshman year that I forever associate him, now, with youth. It was late August, dusk, and hot. The cicadas were out, I remember strangely. The sky was a light shade of pink.

Earlier, the daytime humidity had cracked over Gettysburg, a dry breeze blowing in from the west, settling over our campus and the battlefields both, making everything around us that night look wet: the lines rising off the pavement, the lawn stretching outward toward the dorms. Kevin and I stood as two of seven hundred and fifty freshmen outside Gettysburg College's small, brick church, awaiting the start of the First-Year Walk. It was a tradition nearly a hundred and fifty years in the making, we were told, that began first with Abraham Lincoln in November of 1863.

"This is the event," our orientation guides informed us, "that brings everyone together."

The Civil War was fought in ten thousand engagements as far west as New Mexico and as far north as Vermont. Over three million Americans fought in it, and six hundred thousand—an estimated two percent of the population—died. But in no battle were there more casualties than at Gettysburg, where in the span of three short days—from July 1 to 3, 1863—an estimated 22,638 Confederates and 17,684 Union soldiers were killed or wounded. Nearly eleven thousand more were captured or went missing, and it was that battle, in particular, that changed the outcome of the Civil War.

Had it not been for Gettysburg, American history might well be different.

To this day, it remains the bloodiest conflict to ever occur on U.S. soil, and wasn't it fantastic, we often said, how we attended college on that periphery? Or, more than periphery, really, because during the peak of the engagement, our campus buildings and administrative offices had served as temporary wartime facilities: makeshift hospitals and signaling headquarters. Bodies were stitched up in our basement classrooms, or else were cut open or sawed in half, the discarded, bleeding limbs tossed onto a pile from the lowest windows.

"It's true," a professor told us once, "that many men died where you're now sitting."

They died, too, where we walked and jogged and picnicked. And due to the sheer number of casualties, they remained in those spots for months: against rock walls and rotting fences, under oak trees and in shallow ditches. They lay along creeks and riverbeds, wooded plains, forested hillsides. Our town became a giant graveyard, bodies stiffening in the stifling sun.

But, of course, that wouldn't do—these were men who'd given their lives for a cause the whole nation would soon embrace, so Abraham Lincoln dedicated vast portions of Gettysburg's battlefields to the creation of a new cemetery, the Soldiers' National Cemetery, and the bodies were exhumed and reinterred. Four months later, Lincoln arrived in Gettysburg to march, as if an equal, beside town residents and current students. In the newly dedicated cemetery, he read his Gettysburg Address, surrounded by piles of dirt and the thousands of recently dug, shallow graves.

Remains continued to be found, however: first in 1864, then in 1881, 1899, and even in 1915, fifty-two years after the battle ended, when "remainders of a soldier" were discovered just east of Baltimore Street, one of Gettysburg's busiest roadways. There were just too many bodies, it seemed, to find a proper place for everyone. It wasn't trash that littered Gettysburg; it was bones and bullet shells, and they could be found among blades of grass, or between two twisting, rotting fence posts, or in a shallow gully beside the road.

Every few years, it seemed, a man would plow a field, or he would walk along a hillside, and in these moments he might discover them: a graying rib cage, a fractured skull.

For years following Lincoln's address, the community of Gettysburg and the students of Gettysburg College paid tribute to the fallen soldiers by retracing Lincoln's historic route. They placed wreaths atop the graves, whispered prayers, held moments of silence, but eventually—like anything—this, too, faded into history. Then, in 2003, two years before Kevin and I enrolled, Gettysburg College exhumed the annual walk as part of freshman orientation.

"It's a way of helping students understand where they are," Dean Dennis Murphy explained in an address to the Gettysburg Borough Council. "Students cram everything into their final year; they realize they've been here for four years and have never been on the battlefields."

He was right in one regard: the town's history would only ever be my backdrop—a cartoonish, garish ghost town that sold Confederate lollipops from plastic skulls. It was difficult, even in looking at our quiet campus, to sort the real from the imagined, or to understand Gettysburg as anything more than a place where men abstractly suffered. You could always sense the violence, the static tension in the air, but it never felt close enough. The weight was never there. Forty-six thousand men had died, and above them now we had an Irish bar, a Chinese restaurant, a Dairy Queen. A diner named Ernie's Texas Lunch and a pool where wind pushed limp beach balls and foam noodles across the water, the lights from hotel bedside tables the only lights out there for miles. As students, we laughed about ghosts in upstairs attics, downing shots because we never heard any. We tossed empty beer cans and chunky vomit into the shrubbery lining historic homes, and we rarely—if ever— thought about the bodies as we sat in basement classrooms. We didn't think about their suffering as we played Frisbee in the freshman quad. We referred to that patch of grass, especially, as "Stine Lake," not because it once was one, but because it was there, allegedly, that the amputated limbs of thousands of soldiers had once been burned. Arms, legs, sometimes whole bodies had been piled and lit on fire before decomposition could set in. Over a hundred years later, the soil beneath remained waterlogged and impermeable, so that when it rained hard, it flooded, and we had to swash across in Hunter rain boots.

When it didn't, we all ate sushi and lay flat in bathing suits.

Still, I visited those battlefields often. Some nights, I'd hike to Little Round Top to eat Camembert on water crackers, lean into my boyfriend, drink champagne from a plastic Nalgene. Or I'd hike to Devil's Den to plant myself among the boulders. The sunsets up there were fantastic, far better than anything you could see on campus.

And yet it was the memory of that battle that sustained our tiny town. Gettysburg College, specifically, was made unique by its history—its proximity to the battle and how that nearness made it matter. The East Coast offered dozens of private, liberal arts colleges that boasted small class sizes and safe environments; our student nightclub was one of many and our graduation rate was the same as anyone's.

What set us apart was that violent battle.

And if students didn't care, or if that history felt neglected, Gettysburg became just one of many colleges. In restating that historic tradition—in making seven hundred acne-pocked freshmen march three miles in the blistering heat—our history became just as valuable as our well-manicured flower beds, our eleven fraternities and six sororities, our award-winning dining service and Starbucks cart and homemade pesto. More than our state-of-the-art science center or the sparkling fountain or the observatory. *Did you know our campus library is always open?* read a panel on the school's brochure, and what's more, if you went there after midnight, there was free cocoa served from a mobile cart in the downstairs lobby. We came in our pajamas with our cannon-detailed mugs, and in the gigantic leather chairs on the upper level we drank those beverages slowly, mini marshmallows filming our upper lips. In truth, this always seemed much better than a few old cannons and an obelisk.

And yet the battle. That history. Those double-decker tour buses crawling through our downtown rotary and the women in giant hoopskirts swinging their lanterns from side to side.

Remember who we are, we heard. *Put stock in where you now live.*

"Wear orange and blue to show support," our orientation guides had told us earlier that morning, so we'd spent our afternoon in the campus gift store, holding up athletic shorts and ribbon belts, temporary tattoos and tins of face paint. We squeezed into tiny fitting rooms and pulled the fabric over our legs, admiring our young, toned bodies and striking poses in full-length mirrors.

"Perfect," we agreed. We were so very orange and navy blue.

My friends that first week were a group of tall, lean girls, like women from catalogues. They knew how to French-braid hair and apply eye shadow for a smoky effect, and the only thing we seemed to share was our occupancy on the third floor of Patrick Hall. But still we could all agree on how amazing it was to be at Gettysburg—how with just the swipe of our student ID, the college charged our purchases directly to our parents. So we gathered handfuls of soft, clean merchandise and made our way to the line of registers.

"I'm stocking up," one girl said, holding up a Gettysburg shot glass marked with lines, each labeled with a local college—Franklin & Marshall, Dickinson, Shippensburg— indicating their students could handle only enough liquor to fill up to their line. The top line read GETTYSBURG.

"That's fantastic," another girl said, nodding. "I'm going to send one to my brother—he goes to Franklin & Marshall."

We liked most the idea of being seen: of being a handful of well-dressed women in a crowd of seven hundred. Here were future friends, perhaps the men, we joked, we'd later marry. Maybe we'd meet our soul mates that very night, we said, and then this whole walk would be worthwhile.

"Maybe he's a future doctor," one said, "from a sleepy seaside town that sells great seafood."

"Maybe he's a vet," I said, "and will open his own clinic that he'll let me name."

That night, I wasn't thinking I'd meet a future inmate. I never thought, *This is the start of my prison visits.* I was busy envisioning the name I'd pick: *Caring Tails* or *Paws and Thank You.*

I was imagining men, yes, but only ever the gentle, strong, tan forearms of Gettysburg's upperclassmen, men I hoped would pull me into dark basements or into even darker corners. I imagined ratty couches and ratty futons and the heavy make-out sessions that would inevitably occur there, beneath posters of Bob Marley, atop afghan blankets knit by grandmothers, the bass thumping through the floorboards from the party down below, and how one particular man might hold me tight and say, "It sounds just like my heartbeat."

"I'm wild about you," he'd say, or maybe he'd say nothing to me at all, but later he'd walk me home and point up to the round, white moon, saying my face had never looked prettier than in the cosmic glow of our universe.

"Kiddo," he might call me sweetly.

"He'll have a name like 'Elliot,'" I said. "Or 'Aaron,' or maybe 'Jacob.' Something strong but traditional."

"Not Brett?" one girl said, laughing. "Not Zeke or Riley or Ryder?"

"Absolutely not a Ryder," I said. "No way would I date a Ryder."

I was ready for them—Elliots and Rileys both—and by morning, they'd arrive, showing up with their boxes and BMWs, their leather loafers and khaki board shorts. And with them would come the parties: from Lambda Chi or Sigma Nu, Tau Kappa Epsilon or Phi Sig.

"The parties are usually the same," one girl said, citing secondhand knowledge she swore was hers. "But sometimes there's a concept, with costumes and drinks that fit a theme."

Months earlier, she told us, she'd visited her brother in a

suburb of Boston, and he'd brought her to his fraternity's "Hip-Hop" party.

"All the guys wore fake gold chains," she said, "and the girls tied their shirts in knots. They tattooed their stomachs in the downstairs bathroom with butterflies and baby faces drawn in Sharpie."

There'd probably be a '70s party, she told us, and "Wild West," and "Down on the Farm."

"Each room features a different shot," she said. "Usually Jell-O or tequila, but sometimes vanilla vodka with a lemon wedge."

And it was our right as female freshmen to get through their doors without any questions.

"You can drink all night for free," she said. "The morning hours get especially wild."

But before any of that—before the men, futons, or drinks—there was first this walk, these three historic miles meant to commemorate Gettysburg's honored dead, and it was hot as dusk approached, the heat radiating from the chapel's brick. I hunched over in my orange Polo, fanning my face with an open palm.

"This is kind of silly," I said to no one in particular.

From his place against the doorframe, one student told me to lighten up. "It's important that we do this," he said, "and besides, it won't take long."

I want to say now that I hated this boy, that I found him

condescending and intrusive, and in some ways, I wish I had, because if I'd hated Kevin in that moment, I'd absolve myself from everything that followed. Seven years later, I'd be someone else. But I was bored that night, hot and nervous. I was looking for someone new. The girls on my hall had been fun at first—strange and foreign in how beautiful they were, how easily they secured flavored vodkas and chilled boxed wine—but we had little, if anything, in common. I couldn't make a single braid, for example, and my eyeliner skills were raccoon-like at best.

"Like something positively rabid," one girl said, laughing, pointing to my eyes. "Like bubbles are foaming from your mouth."

These differences would become all the more obvious in the days to follow, when we'd travel together to a small town in Maryland—a place I'd "just have to see"—and in a gravel parking lot beneath a bridge, we'd smoke cigarettes and drink Budweiser tall boys, leaning back dramatically against the car hood. "We're in college now," we'd say, chatting with a group of strange men as they pulled their lines from the deep, black ocean, and when one would offer to take us home—get us high, buy us liquor—I'd say no but the others would say yes, and I'd know then they were not for me.

Already I could sense this: how for weeks we'd be spending our Friday nights in those dank, dark basements of Phi Sig or TKE, not being wooed by some wildly successful, driven man but instead being pushed back against the brick by near-bald men singing "Psycho Killer." We'd hold Solo cups high above our heads, skinny girls pushing past us in black stilettos, and it would be fun for me at first, and then less, and less, and less, and there'd be nearly two hundred photos of us on Facebook, all hugging, holding capped vodkas to open mouths, our lips puffed from snake-venom lipstick, before finally I would admit this. That third night in Gettysburg, however, I was only just beginning to feel uncomfortable, eager for a friendship that didn't rely quite so heavily on a Nikon Coolpix or a miniskirt.

I liked Kevin's sense of duty, as trivial as it would later sound.

"Sorry," I said, embarrassed. "It's just really goddamn hot."

"It's okay," he said, laughing. "I was mostly kidding, anyway."

I don't remember what Kevin was wearing that night or the way he said his name. I don't remember his expression. I don't remember anyone else. What I remember now is just his face: how it was impossibly young and smooth and pale, how his features seemed rounded like a child's. His hair hung between his eyelashes and sweat clung in wet lines across his forehead. His fingers, even, seemed young—how they curled around a cigarette he seemed too sweet to be smoking.

"Nice to meet you," I said, nodding, and then I stood beside him against the brick.

When the walk finally began, I followed Kevin as if by instinct. I know now that we must have marched up Stevens Street, made a left onto Carlisle, crossed through the rotary, and then headed on down Baltimore Street, but that first week in Gettysburg, the streets were anonymous: new, exciting, and unique. We passed souvenir shops and reenactors, kitschy inns and restaurants, and I pointed to their cheap plastic, their dangling flags and wooden rifles.

"Plastic cannons are three for five," I said, nodding. "One for each of us, plus a backup."

In the rotary, we passed a life-size Lincoln statue, tourists clustered in clumps around him. They stuck their fingers up his nose and put their lips on his small, brass cheek.

"Did you get it?" they asked, indignant, cameras clicking wildly along the forefront. "Who knows how many others have kissed this spot."

One middle-aged blonde in a bald eagle T-shirt threw her hands in the air, exasperated.

"You just click that top, round button," she said, "yes, *that one*—that one right there," and her children looked on, silent, as their father stared down dumbly at his disposable camera.

"What a strange, weird place," I said, and Kevin nodded, rolling his eyes.

"You see that?" he said, pointing up to a building I found only ugly, gray, and crumbling. "There are bullet holes in those walls," he said, then, "Jennie Wade died inside that house."

She was the only civilian killed in Gettysburg, he explained, struck dead when a stray bullet pierced her left shoulder before shooting straight into her heart. It came to rest within her corset—"the detail many find most compelling," he said—as she was kneading a ball of dough. It was just eight-thirty in the morning.

"Can you imagine?" he asked, and I did my best to try: I saw her standing in a pleated apron, swatches of flour across

35

her chest, the bullet splintering the pane of glass the way ice cracks beneath two feet.

Kevin told me then he'd been obsessed with the Civil War since childhood, since "before I could talk, probably," he said, and that's why he chose to enroll at Gettysburg.

He said, "I want to be living in a place that matters."

"I just came because they accepted me," I said, "and it's rural, and familiar, and close."

But it stuck out: how even at eighteen, Kevin seemed confident that the things he did could somehow matter—could carry a weight that was all their own. Even that first night, even *then*, he showed a sense of maturity I wanted for myself. There was a whole world inside of Gettysburg, it seemed, full of history and sacrifice, and I felt certain I would learn it if only because of him.

And in many ways, I realize now, that is the truest thing he's taught me.

Inside the Soldiers' National Cemetery, where Lincoln first gave his Address, we took our seats between the tombstones and the soft light of orange dusk. Kevin pulled from the earth dense clumps of clover, tying them neatly into careful loops. Before us, behind a lectern, an Abraham Lincoln impersonator shuffled papers and adjusted his hat.

"That guy actually looks just like him," Kevin said, gesturing toward the front. "I think he's been doing this for years."

"I have a photo with him, I think," I said, "from when I was six, or seven, maybe."

Our makeshift Lincoln was tall, dark, and scrawny, his beard thick and neatly trimmed, but when he cleared his throat and began to read, he embodied our long-gone president. The resemblance resonated throughout the crowd, uncanny and palpable.

"From these honored dead," he read, "we take increased devotion to that cause for which they here gave the last full measure of devotion."

And I could imagine it, suddenly: how it must feel to be just one of six thousand in a small, tight box beneath the earth. It didn't matter how great the cause—you were just a plot of land, no different from the thousands buried beside you, and how tragic that must have been for the loved ones who'd made the visit: to come and see the one you loved, knowing that he is just one of many, that there is nothing you can do.

3

FOR AS COMPLICATED as it has become, our friendship's ori-
gins were in simplicity: I liked Kevin because he liked me,
because he came from a town thirty miles west of mine and
laughed at all my jokes and wore tight T-shirts in solid colors—
red and blue sometimes, but also cranberry, hot pink, purple.
One was baby blue with a cartoon unicorn, its front legs lifted
in a whinnying kick, a rainbow bursting out from somewhere
beneath it to span the length of his thin, flat chest, and Kevin
didn't care what people thought.

He wore that shirt to the grocery store.

Kevin liked writing, drawing, music, most especially the
band Dr. Dog, and in his free time, he remixed rap beats over
pop songs, blending Alicia Keys with Dr. Dre, Rod Stewart
with the Wu-Tang Clan. He posted the tracks to a Myspace
page where he classified the genre as, simply, "euphoric." To
this day, there are over a thousand users who know him only
as DJ Head 'N Shoulders.

What else do I remember? I remember listening to Phish on an autumn morning, the window open; we could see our breath. I remember brownies made from a Ghirardelli mix and clarified marijuana butter, how that smell wafted through the room, impossibly sweet and indulgently pleasant. I remember taking a seat beside Kevin at the long, clean counter of the Lincoln Diner, ordering cup after cup of coffee, and Kevin always first raising the chipped mug to his lips, saying, "Today it tastes like cigarette ash," or "Today it tastes like death."

"Like motor fuel, almost," I'd joke. "Like something thick from inside an engine."

But we didn't mind the taste—that shitty diner and their shitty coffee, burnt and stale and ashy from a morning spent atop the burner. At times, I think, we liked it.

It reminded us of home.

Kevin grew up in Oley, Pennsylvania, a suburb of Reading, home to fewer than four thousand residents. Like my hometown of Telford, Oley is a simple place: the kind where neighbors know neighbors and diners sell scrapple and homemade jams. Companies advertise engagements and newborn babies on street-facing signs—CONGRATULATIONS, ERIC AND TINA! and DEVON, WELCOME TO OUR WORLD!!!—and children play in unfenced yards. Family businesses stay in families. Kevin's own parents managed a grocery store, where he used to work in high school.

"I stocked shelves," he told me once. "I was too shy to work the register."

I know these details because I've been there—because I saw those things for myself. I've walked through that narrow supermarket and bought an apple and I said nothing, though I looked at *that* man and *that* man and *that* man, searching for some resemblance. I drove, too, past many homes and peered into each backyard, trying to imagine my friend as a child and wondering at what point exactly his innocence turned.

I looked into bedroom windows, at timers clicking on evening sprinklers, and I've done this, however strangely, because of our shared origin. It is what unsettles me the most. In truth, the snacks we ate as children were likely identical; the shows we watched, the music we played. Our parents, who were firm but loving, hardworking, intelligent, middle-class. I imagine his bedroom like it's my own; his neon sneakers like mine, but larger. His hair washed in the same shampoo.

Something had turned inside of Kevin, and I want to know if it could turn inside me, too.

Kevin and I had both come to Gettysburg, in fact, because we enjoyed familiarity in all things—friendship, certainly, but also landscapes, geography. It would be easy now to say it was the school's strong reputation we liked, how it was private and top-ranking, but it was something else entirely: We liked that the small town that contained Gettysburg College was so similar to the smaller towns where we were from. In Gettysburg, or Oley, or Telford, we had a record store and a coffee shop, a Chinese restaurant and a few dim dive bars. The restaurants were mostly booths, always carpeted, and lined with wallpaper: girls holding hands with young, thin boys, or ducks chasing ducklings across a pond. Even the entrées were predictable—chicken fried steak, biscuits with gravy—and named after the patrons who ordered them the most.

Bob's Favorite Chicken Fried Steak.

The *French Toast à la Lincoln.*

There or elsewhere, we had flea markets, and pancake breakfasts, and Friday night fish fries at the American Legion. There were antique-car shows held in parking lots, whole families sitting in vinyl lawn chairs, the grass beneath them dry from where idling children had scuffed their shoes. The adults drank Mountain Dew and licked vanilla soft-serve from kiddie cones, and the kids were all the same: plain, but lovely in their own way.

Gettysburg afforded the luxury of similarity with the thrill of being new: a McDonald's like ours but *different*, a bookstore like ours but *different*.

We liked, too, the allure of the battlefields, the history, the way thousands of people came to our town each year to take pictures and buy postcards of the place we called our home. We didn't mind the Boy Scouts caravanning in navy blue minivans, the women hanging from the backs of motorcycles, their big hair shining in the sun. We didn't mind the haunted ghost tours rattling through our empty acres, their tour guides yelling dates and numbers that only echoed across the dry, flat land. Twice a year, the KKK arrived to hand out booklets as small as my palm, and we watched as families with out-of-state license plates drove by slowly, clicking their cameras at the men's white caps. It was the most danger we ever faced—more a threat of suggestion than physical harm. In Gettysburg, we never had to worry about catching a taxi, or getting mugged, or even getting lost. It was a place where we could grow, experience college and then life beyond it:

in Boston or Denver or San Francisco, in New York City or L.A.

"Soon, I'll live in a place with concert halls," Kevin once said, "and live music every night."

"I'm going to live in a building with a lobby," I said, "a front desk, and a key code."

It was our mutual fantasy: this idea of abstract bigness. In four years' time, Kevin and I would graduate and leave Gettysburg. We would leave Oley, and leave Telford, and leave all of Pennsylvania. Chicago or Miami—what happened next didn't really matter, so long as it was bigger and brighter than the places we'd always known.

"It's hard to learn a new city," Kevin said, "so it seems smart to stay small for now."

I think in some way we needed Gettysburg, too, to hone the idea of our future selves. Kevin and I had both been raised in relatively easy, carefree households, and what art could we ever create, we joked, from cartoon shows about adventuring aardvarks? From weekend breakfasts of heart-shaped eggs? My mother had prepared daily after-school snacks of fresh fruit and nuts and raisins, Granny Smith apples arranged as a face with cheese, and what sad or longing poetry could I ever create from that?

"I mean, we ran out of apples from time to time," I joked, "but that was pretty much it."

"My mother once took a second job," Kevin said, "but I just looted the cabinets for fruit snacks."

Gettysburg was to be our creative muse, safe in familiarity while new enough to encourage exploration, and so when finally we reached our new city—wherever that might be—we thought we'd be richer for the experience. We'd finally have something to say. And so it goes without saying, perhaps, that when I imagined my distant future after graduation, I imagined Kevin as some small part of it. I saw us passing well-lit storefronts and rows of food stalls, vendors in paper hats trying to sell us sausages and sweet peppers, hot dogs wrapped in day-old buns. Women in red galoshes would walk dogs in yellow raincoats, their paws padding softly across wet concrete, and men in herringbone or tweed would drink brown beverages from sweating glasses. Our city—whichever city—would hum with the static of a million people, and we'd hum right there among them, two of them at last.

"To getting out," I'd say to Kevin, clinking my glass against his at a table along a harbor. We would work jobs in office complexes, date city people in long black coats who knew nothing of small-town life or the Civil War or Gettysburg. This is what we preferred—we assumed our new urban roles quickly—and in restaurants high above the sidewalks, we would order saffron risotto with wild mushrooms and entrées of delicately prepared blue crab, and we'd return to Gettysburg only for reunions or the overdue weddings of college friends.

"How nice to be back," we'd say, and whether or not we meant it always seemed arbitrary.

But Kevin never moved to San Francisco, not to New Orleans or Tallahassee. We never spent an afternoon at a Brooklyn street fair; I never saw his concert or went backstage. We never moved to a big, bright city or ate in restaurants with river views.

I left Gettysburg—that much is true—but for two years, Kevin stayed: first in a solitary-confinement cell and then in a general-holding wing just five miles away from our former college, where the distant view from his only window was of the mountains we used to hike. All of our friends graduated and moved away: one north to Boston, one to California. One left the country to teach in Seoul, and one returned to New York City. In Napa Valley, Eric opened a restaurant where he sells grits and honeydew salad. He sends me postcards from the wineries, writes, *I am drunk*, and signs his name.

But in Gettysburg, Pennsylvania, Kevin awaited trial. I visited him there only once, driving the hundred and thirty miles west from Telford after a nine-hour shift folding jeans in the local mall. I remember only the pavement—loud beneath my tires—and how I bit my lip until it bled, a nervous habit retained since childhood. In Gettysburg, I sat across from Kevin at a booth, a slab of glass between us, and watched as I picked up a telephone while, inches away, he did the same—my mirror image, both of us twenty-two, of normal build and normal height, except I wore jeans and a red T-shirt and he wore the state-issued uniform: a button-down beige cotton jumpsuit.

"How is it?" I asked, never using the word *prison*.

"How do you feel?" I asked, never adding, "Now that she's dead?"

"We're in a heat wave," I said instead, unsure if he even knew in prison.

"Good," he said, and "All right," and "That's what everyone is saying."

Our hour ended and I drove to the campus. I walked the passageways we used to walk and entered classrooms where once we'd learned. We'd spent hours inside those buildings, imagining the distant day when we would leave them, because what, we often joked, could possibly keep us here?

In the grass outside the library, I sat on the bench they'd bought for her.

Along the back is her full name, and in the mulch, pinwheels like daisies.

There were daisies alongside the highway, too, the first time I thought to visit him in this prison, three months before this November morning. I'd spent that week visiting family in New Hampshire, sunning on a floating dock in the middle of a lake, and my route home took me ten miles from Albion. Of course I thought of him: saw him rising from his cot to look out at the visitors' parking lot from a window barricaded by thick, barred glass, one I wasn't certain he even had. And if he did, who's to say he'd see me? Or that he'd know it was me and not someone else?

But still, I pictured him there, waiting.

He'd see my car and maybe recognize it, though it's been years since he saw it last. *Amy*, he'd think, *she's here!* and I hoped that surprise might feel wonderful.

But I wasn't certain he was allowed to have visitors yet—it had been only a month since his relocation. It seemed a risk to even try. Instead, I watched on my GPS as Kevin's downtown disappeared, out there in the distance, the small pinpoint I wrote to often. My car sped across the freeway, past Costco and BJ's and Sam's Club, and for the seconds that they were in sight, I thought, *I wonder how far this is from Kevin's world.*

How far this. *How far* this: these symbols of prosperity, commerce, giant warehouses he'll never enter, selling their twenty-ounce bottles of A.1. steak sauce and twelve-packs of Near East rice.

Sometimes I squirt ketchup into my Ramen Noodles, he wrote once. *I like to pretend I'm at the Vietnamese restaurant.* The restaurant was just a shack and a splintered picnic table, no more than eighty yards from the freeway, but we went each week for months until the night of his arrest.

And I get a hamburger once a year, he wrote, *in honor of the Fourth of July.*

But because there is no announcement or special stationery or the ability to order a cake from outside a prison—and I know, because I've looked—his birthdays always go unnoticed.

But it's easier this way, he wrote.

A birthday means another year, and another year means he has at least twenty-four more.

From my car, I could see those warehouse parking lots— the highway ran just above them—and they were filled to capacity with minivans, SUVs, mothers pushing frozen tilapia and lobster tails in carts to cars. The truck beds contained flat-screen TVs held down by jumper cables, and tables and Blu-ray players, standing lamps, and video games.

These fucking people and all their shit, I thought. *They should be the ones in jail.*

Kevin owns none of what these people think they need: giant jars of mayonnaise, MacBook Pros. His only possessions are a spiral-bound notebook, a ballpoint pen, an FM radio. And if he were in any other Pennsylvania prison—SCI Graterford, SCI Houtzdale—he'd have at least five or six stations to choose from; in all likelihood, he'd have quite a few more. But in Albion, Pennsylvania, he's lucky if he can pull in three. On a good day, he says, five.

Those people and their carts—they had iPads and quesadilla makers, hot-milk frothers, travel mugs. They had *Shrek 2*, and *Up*, and *Titanic*. They had *Jackass* in 3-D.

It's good you decided not to visit, Kevin wrote in response when I later told him. *It'll take you months to get on the visitors list, but it's nice you thought of me.*

But now, of course, I'm on it. I've sent the prison a copy of my driver's license, my social security number and home address, and what this means—the only thing that matters—is that I can now enter his prison's lobby.

"I'm a friend of Kevin Schaeffer's," I'll say. "I've come all the way from Iowa."

I'll hand the guards my ID as if it's proof of how much I care: three holographic windmills that explain why I never visit, my street four states away, across the Mississippi, even. "It's my first time," I'll say, thinking, *There's no way that you can blame me.*

I'll pass through their two large doors, head down one

hallway and then another, and then in an open-air cafeteria—no different from the one I used in high school—I'll see Kevin walking toward me, his arms outstretched, as if nothing's changed.

And if my hour of preparation in the hotel bathroom will do—*can do*—anything, it will convince him that it hasn't.

"Do you know what I think is nice?" I remember Kevin asking once. It was our fourth Saturday on campus, the first cool day of the impending fall, and we were sitting at the Lincoln Diner, stabbing translucent eggs with our forks' bent prongs.

"What?" I asked.

"How at least there are people like us," he said. "That no matter who else is here, at least we have each other."

What he meant were who we considered the rest of the college campus: men in lobster belts and women in paisley prints and neon heels. He meant their jewelry and Connecticut accents, their big blond ponytails, teased and sprayed.

"Sure," I said, simply, because I didn't want to repeat those words. It was my experience—however small—that my male friends often developed feelings for me if I hung around too much, not because I was pretty or funny or sweet, or anything other than indulgent with my company.

I didn't like to be alone.

And often, this wasn't a problem, because I always hung out in groups—it was always me, and then some guy, and some other girl, and some other guy—but in Gettysburg those first few weeks, we were more or less alone. And of course I laughed at all his jokes. Of course I texted him when I was lonely.

"It's a good friendship," I said, nodding.

In fact, it was easy, those first few weeks, to disregard the college's social scene—the fraternity parties and sorority girls and the recurring soundtrack of O-Zone's "Numa Numa"—because *at least we had each other*. Instead, we spent those nights watching documentaries in basement classrooms, janitors eyeing us through the glass, and when Kevin took a job at the campus library—where he learned that students could check out projectors—he drove east to get his PlayStation, and we began playing rented video games against our dorm room walls. We'd throw women from speeding cars, shoot at policemen until they fell, watch their pulsating bodies suffer, life-size and bleeding across the brick.

"It's kinda fucked up if you think about it," he said once, and I said, "I don't know why you would."

I didn't want a reason to turn them off or put them on pause or put them away. I liked their graphic nature: how detailed and how lifelike, how sensational and overtly violent. The way the women in the video games looked like sleeker, stronger versions of the woman I hoped to be.

We'd play for hours, and later, exhausted and overstimulated, we'd walk to the 7-Eleven to buy bags of chips in curious flavors.

"Dannnnngerously cheesy!" Kevin would say, holding up a bag of flavor-blasted Cheetos. He'd shake his body like a Tasmanian devil, saying, "I can hardly handle the *cheeeeeeese!*"

We ate them in the quiet quad to a steady stream of sorority sisters returning home from their basement parties. They moved delicately in dense, narrow packs, their high heels clicking loudly across the sidewalk. They held their cell phones out in front of them, like inefficient flashlights, and stumbled like baby birds, disoriented, raising their arms and crying out when finally their legs gave out beneath them.

"They're so cute when they're small," I'd say, laughing, and Kevin would say, "You're giving them too hard a time."

But by mid-October, our isolation seemed nothing if not lonely. We weren't preserving ourselves so much as sequestering, keeping ourselves away from potential companions, so when one Saturday Kevin and I noticed students occupying a back booth of the Lincoln Diner—seven of them in all—I said, "They don't look like assholes." I said, "They look pretty cool."

"I bet they don't go to frats," Kevin said. "I bet they don't give a shit."

They looked worn-in in a way we liked: dressed in T-shirts creased with sweat, jeans with holes, shoes with scuffs. And when we craned our necks to hear their conversation, it was quintessential in its college-coolness: Raymond Carver and Jack Kerouac and one girl's experience with evangelism.

"That shit fucked my childhood *up*," she said. "I escaped religion only through literature."

"Jack Kerouac is the fucking man," another agreed. "Everyone only talks about *On the Road* when *Dharma Bums* is where it's really at."

And of course we loved them instantly. Later, after they left, we followed behind, pretending to smoke.

"Hold up," I said, reaching my arm out in front of Kevin. "We don't want to make it too obvious."

"Sure," he said, "you're right." He bent down to fake retying a sneaker.

We watched from a distance as they filed first through a narrow alleyway beside a church and then past an old, brick, narrow building. It was tall and thin and bordered by dumpsters. Paint peeled from the rusting fire escape—big chips that flaked off like skin and collected in the potted planters down below.

"That's off-campus housing," I said, because it was uncommon in Gettysburg; over the years, the administration had purchased nearly every building within a five-block radius with the intent of housing their students closely. Proximity was important, but so, too, was supervision. We were prohibited from owning candles or hot pots or incense, to say nothing of beer or wine.

"I bet they can do anything they want," I said. "Smoke weed, burn a fat jar of birthday cake, or warm vanilla sugar, or evergreen."

"Pretty fucking cool," Kevin agreed. "I bet inside, that place is awesome."

It was easy, before we met them, to feel proud of the life we'd made—how it was familiar and yet new, how we'd carved it from a space so small that everyone else just drank and danced. But still we envied their unity. How at least they had each other. We envied even the sound of them: Van Morrison and glass clinked on glass.

I imagined taking a seat beside them on intricate tapestries spread across the rooftop, flicking cigarette butts over railings, smoking hookah from a big, brass pipe. The air would blow cool and sweet as it mixed with diesel exhaust and dusty gravel, and we'd listen as bells chimed from the bed-and-breakfast a block away.

"That place is pocked with bullet shells," Kevin would tell me, and then we'd turn the music up, our attempt to block the bell's brassy noise.

When days later I met Keith—and recognized him instantly from their group—of course I began to date him. It happened almost immediately. Friday nights, he'd invite me over to cook dinner and listen to records, and I never hesitated to ask about Kevin: if maybe he could join us, too.

"He's good people," I said. "You'll like him," and Keith said sure, that was fine.

"We've all got to stick together," he said, "living in a place like this."

And it was all too easy to believe then that what happened in Gettysburg would unite us all for life.

All I remember of that building now is that it was cool inside and sparsely lit. The hallways were lined with posters—naked women, AC/DC, Hiroshima's mushroom cloud—and they kept the doors propped open with wine bottles, vintage books, and Hindu statues.

"So everyone can come and go as they please," Keith explained. "We have a free visiting policy."

Some nights, we cooked food—honeyed ham, brownies with caramel, whole pots of curried chicken—then climbed up to the rooftop to turn the floodlights on, lie across tapestries on our backs, point out stars as double-decker tour buses rattled far below. Other nights, we sat along someone's floor and passed around a bottle of something strong. Each apartment had its own record player and a milk crate full of albums. There were the Beatles, James Taylor, the Grateful Dead, Bob Dylan, Phish. My favorite was Donovan's "Wear Your Love Like Heaven," because it made me feel nearly weightless.

"It's like I'm floating on a goddamn cloud," I'd say, "somewhere high above the earth."

"It's incredible," Kevin said once, nodding. "I agree— fucking fantastic."

Each night, we sat there in some stunned silence, imagining the melodies floating in the air above as if tangible and real—moving first through empty hallways and then our campus and those battlefields—and later, on the long walk home, I'd gush to Kevin about how I felt grateful.

"That we found them," I always said. "That we found people who are just like us."

"Definitely," he'd say. "I'm definitely glad that we met them."

But Kevin and I were different from our new group in one key way, a way that mattered at eighteen, however silly it might seem now. Each member of that house had experienced what I thought of as a "defining difficulty": a bitter parental divorce, an oppressive religion, an abusive or otherwise absent father. Two had sat before judges and picked which parent they would live with, and another was forced to move around so much she got anxious, she said, if she bought *anything*.

"Just one more thing to have to move," she'd said, so she owned only what could fit into boxes: a few cotton tank tops, an old sweater, a pair of shoes, some holey jeans.

From what I could tell, Kevin and I knew nothing of that loss, that difficulty, of any true or tangible struggle. We'd never experienced anything graver, it seemed, than a verbal altercation or a romantic rejection in a junior high hallway. Our parents were still together and our childhoods, for the most part, had been peaceful. Our grandmothers were still alive and sent us Snoopy-themed birthday cards each year in the mail.

"My parents really love each other," Kevin said once. "I knew nothing but that security."

"Mine still have romantic suppers on the moonlit porch," I said, "where they eat seafood and tiny, artisanal noodles."

Every night we sat in that building, I felt more and more conscious of our privilege, our good fortune, my brand-name jacket and ballet flats. Even the locket I wore—even *that* was a symbol of my security. My parents had given it to me the day I left for Gettysburg, and inside my mother had secured a heart-shaped cutout of the family dog with Elmer's glue.

"That way you won't ever forget who's at home waiting," she said, "or sleeping on the pillows on top of your bed."

So I was grateful that I had Kevin—he made me feel a little less alone. We shared a secret, shared a connection, a quiet understanding of how blessed we'd been. *It's as if you and I were the lucky chosen*, he wrote once, *to be part of that great group of people*. So even after months passed and we learned these friends better, even after I fell in love with Keith and spent less time with Kevin, even as whole years began to pass, and we changed, and I became no closer to him than anyone, it was something we still had in common: how we'd been lucky, so far, in life.

4

AND HE IS LUCKY EVEN NOW, I think as my car cuts across the countryside toward the prison, the sun like yolk across the fields. Dawn has broken wet above the valley, and the light bends iridescent over wheat and sweet corn, frayed cobs decomposing in the tilled, dull dirt. I roll the windows down and decide that it is nice. *It's nice,* I think, *he's here.* Thirty years in quiet America, a place where fields stretch outward, where he can breathe and clear his head.

I flip on the radio, where a man is singing about a country town he wants to escape. *Gotta get out of here,* he sings, *get it all off my mind,* while in mine, I'm imagining Albion, realizing how—in just mere minutes—I will see it for the first time. In the months leading up to Kevin's relocation, I've tried to imagine it as a place with movie-rental stores and hair salons, banks and car washes and Dairy Queens. Fathers leading daughters through aisles of small-town grocery stores, and mothers pushing strollers, babies strapped to their backs or fronts.

A place similar, in ways, to Gettysburg, because that much once seemed important.

What I wanted, more than anything, was to imagine Kevin's view—to know he could look from his small cell window to see something beautiful along its edge: a blinking downtown in the distance, a well-lit corner on his horizon. It wouldn't be New York City or even Boston, but maybe at night he could pretend.

And yet I never wanted to know—not really, anyway. I spent my evenings zooming in and out on Google Earth, recognizing Kevin's facility first as an orange dot surrounded by plots of undeveloped land—all of them green or gold and empty—but then, with just a click, I could zoom in to make out more: first the wing where I knew he was kept, then the chain-link fence, and finally the two running tracks on the property's northern side.

Another click and I could see people, and I'd always pretend that one was Kevin.

He's playing basketball today, I'd think, or *There he is, at the picnic table.*

I live inside the fantasy because it's better than the alternative. I cannot imagine my friend sitting in a cell, solitary and alone. Some nights, I imagine him holding a plastic knife, the kind they give him at every meal. It is a knife meant for frozen pizza or a baked potato, and it is dull, but still I imagine him carving it somehow, flicking the plastic against the cinder block of his cell until it is clean and sharp and smooth. I see him pressing it into his skin, so thin and white as paper, and I imagine him scraping, digging, carving.

I think, *By the time I finally visit my friend, he will no longer be alive.*

I have no way of knowing, however, whether my concerns about his safety or health are legitimate. We never talk about what happened; we never talk about that night or how he felt as it unfolded. During his initial incarceration in Gettysburg, Kevin was forced to see a therapist—someone to coach him through the process, this strange and new lifestyle—and she was supposed to make it easier, but it seemed she only ever made him angry. In the only letter he ever sent that acknowledged an ongoing situation, he noted that she'd diagnosed him with depression, feared he might be suicidal.

Do you believe her? he wrote. *Of course I'm depressed, living in a place like this.*

But I have no way of knowing if he is seeing anyone now in Albion, or if he's provided with the "support as needed," as it states in his prison intake file. He doesn't talk to me about what matters—certainly not illness and never what happened, only Scrabble and the words he plays.

"Placate," he writes. *It used up all my tiles!*

So he is playing basketball, I tell myself, or lying on a picnic table—something familiar to him, if new. He is surrounded by open fields, casting his gaze upward, drawing animals from the swollen sky, imagining not brutality at all but a rhinoceros, a hippopotamus.

I've explored his lonely corner of Pennsylvania, as well, making note of the Pennsylvania exits he'll likely see on the morning of his release, twenty-six years from this autumn sunrise. The towns have names that I think sound pleasant: North Springfield and Avonia, Harborcreek and Lake City.

Lake City, I think, *sounds nice.*

I picture gray slate and white crystals, rocks the color of gemstones dredged from the bottom of Lake Erie. I imagine sifting fistfuls of that sand, running my fingers over the edge to reveal colored glass rubbed smooth. I've pictured lily pads, for whatever reason, and tiny green and brown speckled frogs. I've never seen Lake Erie, but after my visit, perhaps I will— pick up a sandwich at a local deli and dip my feet into the clear, cool water. *The Erie*, I'll think, *how lovely*, and won't I be relieved? That all of this is over? That it was successful *but now it's over?*

So Albion will be like Lake City, I think, or exactly like Harborcreek—these places that sound like postcards or the covers of retail calendars. And yet when finally I arrive, it is nothing like what I've wanted. It is smaller and quieter than Oley. It is smaller, even, than Gettysburg.

The only movement I can spot is contained within a barber's pole.

A sign outside a gas station reads 2-FOR-1 RED AND GREEN

SLURPEES!, and there are two pumps, though one is broken, a plastic bag tied clumsily around its handle.

But the Slurpees are Christmas-themed, I think, and in some small way, I guess that's nice. But here is what I find myself thinking: *Did he like Slurpees, whatever color? Will he buy one the day of his release?* I imagine him on a bus, if indeed a bus arrives to shepherd inmates from that prison to the rest of the world, the rest of their lives. In the movies, I know they do. I picture Kevin leaning against the glass as the bus startles into motion, traversing the very road I find myself on this autumn morning. It's a ridiculous line of questioning—to crave or not crave a Slurpee—but feels important for me to know.

That I cannot recall even the simplest things about Kevin, about what he likes, about what he dislikes—even despite my many letters, how they span many months—feels, in ways, pejorative. I prefer to think that Kevin and I were always close, but in truth, I use that term loosely; there are several people, in fact, who to this day might argue Kevin and I were not close friends at all, and it could be argued that they are right. In Gettysburg, ours was a social circle of nine or ten people, always with an array of rotating boyfriends and girlfriends orbiting our periphery, and Kevin was simply one of nine whose faces remained consistent over the years. But those years as college students, he was no closer to me than Eric was. No closer than Sam or Tiffany or Cass, Andrew, Ben, or James.

And yet I knew Kevin. I trusted him.

Once, in a bedroom filled with oriental throw rugs, we blew bubbles using an oversized wand, the kind sold in dollar stores. "Watch this," Kevin said lightly, inserting his cigarette into the film. He blew shallow, quiet breaths and, together, we watched the gray and shining gases rise slowly within glossy rainbows.

"Beautiful," I said.

On another occasion, Kevin baked me Bagel Bites at three a.m. because I was drunk—too drunk, he claimed, for bed. He said, "You'll feel awful in the morning." He waited beside me at the kitchen table until every single one was gone.

So I was not Kevin's best friend, no, but *a* friend, a person who cared for him, and in the days and weeks following what he did, it seems that care somehow compounded. But now, however, on this drive to his prison, I'm suddenly aware of that disconnect: how, in truth, I grew closer to him only after his violent crime. And what I fear most about this visit is not how I anticipate he will make me feel, but how it feels when I realize—for the first time—that, in person, we're nearly strangers. After all, the person Kevin remembers is not a person I can even pretend to be. Kevin remembers me at twenty-two—a twig of a girl who tied her shoes with neon laces and painted her nails to look like rainbows. I used a series of wooden toothpicks, dipping each one in a different polish. I wore cheap jewelry from mall boutiques—pearls painted pink, bronze and silver chandeliers—and cooked my eggs in flower molds.

"I don't eat anything with a face," I said often, and I made my father use a different spatula to flip my Boca Burger patty.

Now I eat nearly anything. Because I've been in what Kevin refers to as the "real world" for three years, I now look and dress and sound—and, of course, *of course* I think—differently from my college self, and much of this, I know, is a result of what he did. I don't care, anymore, about trapping and releasing a spider. I don't have the energy to illustrate my nails. I eat steak because of its strength, the way I imagine its power rushes back into my flesh.

But for the many ways I've changed, Kevin, it seems, remains the same; in nearly every letter he writes, he includes illustrations of tiny kittens, bouquets of flowers, a sun in sunglasses—the same sketches he used to doodle in my margins in our college classrooms. *I love you beary much*, two hugging bears told me last winter, and it was all I could think to do to pin them to my fridge with a Red Lobster magnet.

Now they're the first thing I see each morning as I pour my coffee or slice an orange.

I love you beary much.

Kevin remains stunted, in other words, proverbially twenty-two, and if he were any other college friend, our reunion would be easy; I would sit across from him at a table and explain my life through bullet points.

"Here's what I've been up to," I'd say, and then he would say the same.

But of course Kevin is not working in Washington, D.C., not Boston, not even Pittsburgh. He is not going to new restaurants or trying new foods or attempting new things. He is not going or doing or visiting anywhere beyond the confines of his big gray prison. The majority of his days are spent in an eight-by-ten cell, where his wardrobe never changes and even his time is carefully managed: two hours every afternoon to go outside and dribble a basketball, with evenings reserved for reading, writing letters, and playing Scrabble.

The guys all think I cheat, he wrote once, *because they don't know the words I play.*

During his initial incarceration inside the Adams County Correctional Center in Gettysburg, in fact, Kevin confided he was the only one who was college-educated, and it was this, he thought, more than anything else, that caused him difficulty in making friends. In one particularly upsetting story he told me, he spent a day in "the hole"—a solitary-confinement cell—for playing a word in Scrabble that the guard claimed did not exist. *Why didn't he look it up?* I thought, but knew this was likely beside the point.

Kevin remembers with fondness, then, our friendship—not his and mine exclusively, but all the many he once shared. And yet because these relationships never evolved past the confines of Gettysburg College's careful campus, they never grew up or moved away or changed their shape into something adult. And now there is no other way to think about how we once spent our Friday nights—it was *crazy* to drive thirty miles through empty battlefields and unfolding farmland, over the Mason-Dixon Line, past the mountains, to a liquor store in Maryland that sold its champagne bottles three-for-ten.

It was crazy—how we bought them in bulk and lined them like infants across our backseat, cushioning them with free beach towels from local banks and old T-shirts and picnic blankets.

It is embarrassing to remember how we later poured them

into plastic fishbowls, added toy fish from the Dollar General, and drank from them at parties with looping, neon-green Krazy Straws.

Those were the best days of my life, Kevin wrote once, *and I didn't even know it.*

Because I am not in prison, I fear Kevin thinks this is the life that I still live: eating Chinese food at midnight, soaking cubed watermelon in vodka. We knew each other during a period of time in which whole days could pass without needing to change out of sweatpants; when one semester I arranged my schedule carefully so as to have my Thursdays through Mondays off. I spent them in pajamas, doing homework and baking cookies. HOTTIE, one pair read, and I wore them out when I ran errands: standing in line at the local post office, buying bananas at the grocery store.

I knew absolutely nothing of loss.

At the only traffic light in Albion, I make a left and pass a post office. I pass ranch-style homes and a dog kennel, and finally, the sprawling cemetery, and I know that I am close.

How strange, I thought when I first saw it, scanning Google Earth on a wintry morning. I was sitting in my sunlit apartment in Iowa, and from the other side of the wall, I could hear a tenant's shower going, the familiar beep of a microwave. I pushed back and away from the computer, thinking, *Of all the things to put him beside.*

A cemetery, for fuck's sake.

Nearly anything would've been better: a car dealership, a nail salon. To put Kevin beside a cemetery is to remind him daily of what he did, and while some might argue for that as punishment, Kevin already carries that heavy burden.

"I wish it was me every single day," he read from his speech the day of his sentencing. "I see her face, and I'm so sorry."

And now he looks at graves, I think, pulling my car into the parking lot. I pull my keys from the ignition and do an inventory of what I see: the cemetery and beat-up Hondas, a big blue mailbox, a fire hydrant.

It reminds me of a road-trip game my friends and I play in Iowa. We call it simply "the counting game," and the idea of it is this: Before the drive begins, we agree upon a list of random objects that, when spotted, count and accumulate as points. Oftentimes, the things my friends and I pick are simple and fairly common: stars on barns, riding mowers, bird feeders, boxers hung on a line to dry. Each counts for a point. Yellow Cabs, a popular eighteen-wheeler company, also count for a single point, but a frozen-pizza truck—DiGiorno or Palermo's—ends the game on sight. This is what you do when everything around you looks the same, when flatness and stagnation are the only attributes of the moving landscape. You make an effort to notice subtlety; you make a game of differentiating.

The first time we played, we agreed flags would be plentiful, and a minute later, I spotted one painted across the façade of a red barn. I saw another on a pole outside a school. There were Yellow Cabs in rest-stop parking lots, men in baseball caps riding lawn mowers. Our car sped across I-80, past housing developments and trailer parks, and for the seconds they were in sight, I snuck a peek into each backyard.

Once, in Elkhart, Indiana, I looked up at the split image of a heart painted across a water tower, thinking it was a flag. My eyes seized on the red and blue, the breaking the white presented; its colors were all the same, but it was a different shape entirely. It was a heart: half red, half blue, with thick, white lines splitting the familiar figure. It took seconds for me to realize the white lines formed an animal, not a rupture.

"I thought it was a broken heart," I offered. "I thought it was split right down the middle."

"It's an *elk*," my friend said, pointing out the shape of the antlered animal.

"Oh," I said, wondering why pain was my first instinct.

In Albion, in my quiet car, I feel that pain again. From the front of the prison, a flag the size of a bedsheet ripples limply in the autumn wind, and I think to call it out, but of course there is no one but me to count it.

Inside, the woman I approach is exactly as I've imagined—her skin shiny and without powder, her hair held back in a glossy ponytail. Her lips and outfit match, their color nude, like compact sand.

"Hi," I say, not knowing what else to say. "I'm here for Kevin Schaeffer?"

She keeps her eyes fixed beneath us but points to a pad of paper. Here is a grid already half full with the names and identifying information of the people waiting behind us in bucket seats.

"You'll want to fill this out," she says, so I write my name, address, and phone number, then my social security number and the date. "Inmate number?" she asks when she sees I've left that blank.

"I don't know," I say. "JT-something. I don't remember the exact specifics."

In the three years since Kevin's arrest, I've written him several dozen letters, each marked carefully with this particular code, but still I cannot remember it, as if my mind refuses to replace his name with his new state-issued identification. He is *Kevin Schaeffer*, the boy who lived in the freshman dorm across from mine. *Kevin Schaeffer*, history major and honors student and president of the college radio station. *Kevin Schaeffer*, who walked me home the same night *Kevin Schaeffer Pleads Guilty to Fatally Stabbing Fellow Student*.

"I'll look it up," the woman says, typing into her computer.

In the waiting room, I take my seat and cannot help but examine the others waiting. These are elderly couples, children, one woman done up with a lot of makeup and hair spray. She is the face I've long imagined when I tried to picture a prison visit: the sad wife who cannot grasp her new reality, who so clearly cannot deal with the fact that her husband now resides inside a maximum-security prison. The woman on PrisonTalk.com who claims it's not the worst thing in the world to have to go in without a bra.

He really likes it, she wrote. *It gives him a sort of thrill.*

He is a criminal, I think, looking up at her from my seat. I am different from her, I know, because Kevin is and only ever was a friend. At times, I make this obvious: I leave his letters on my kitchen table, available for anyone to see. Normally, I try to hide them—under the fruit basket, in a filing cabinet— but every now and then, I decide it's good that people know. I have absolutely nothing to hide.

"Oh, these?" I say, shrugging. "Just an old friend, but we've kept in touch."

I am, in fact, the only one who has, though I am not—and this is important—the only one who thinks of Kevin. I imagine without really knowing that Kevin is likely the rea- son Eric moved to California, or why he doesn't return my messages, or why—when I call him on his birthday—the phone rings once and then clicks to voicemail. It seems to me Kevin is the reason Etta works in a women's shelter, why Helen moved to Colorado, why Sam—a former philosophy major—has made a career out of saving lives.

"It was a hard decision," he told me once, "but going to med school just feels right."

Tim now kayaks on his every lunch hour, claiming it's important we make the best of the time we have, and Keith seeks out culinary pleasure—the simplest, the most resolute, the taste of peas on a tongue. But I have no way of knowing if Kevin is why one of us left to teach in South Korea, why another spent a year volunteering in Africa. There is no way for me to prove that Kevin, in fact, is why Leslie got married in the Kentucky countryside, a string of hot-air balloons rising slowly above her, their spherical shadows like apparitions, and why when I sat in a foldout chair and watched it, I thought, This *is how love should work.*

It's not that we didn't care, necessarily, about these people or pursuits prior to that April night, but in many ways, it seems to me Kevin made us hold on to things a little bit tighter, press our loved ones a little bit closer, like children clutching candy, saying, *Please do not take these things from us.*

And yet aside from his aging parents, an aunt, and one cousin, I am the only one who writes Kevin regularly, much less takes the time to visit. I am his only remaining link to normalcy, the only person not indebted to him by blood.

You remember me for who I was, he wrote once, *not who I've become in these last three years.*

I've packed quarters for microwavable pizzas, Cherry Coke, and Tastykakes.

And this woman in her bucket seat—I am nothing in the world like her. Her face so clean and smooth. Her lips outlined with liner.

I miss you, I imagine she writes, desperate to be with her husband without a guard.

What are you reading? I write to Kevin. *How's the weather out there in Albion?*

5

MY SUREST MEMORIES of that April night are of a phone conversation and an acrylic painting of a parrot. The conversation came first: I stood on the condemned fire escape spanning the length of my apartment and crooned to Kevin that the sky was pink. "Red sky at night, sailor's delight," I said, "and doesn't that mean it's a sign? That we should go celebrate?"

From his place on the other end of the line—a cubicle in the campus library—Kevin sounded lethargic, distant, as if it weren't two blocks that separated us but a country, a continent, an entire universe, which I realize now it might as well have been. There might as well have been ornate cathedrals between us, houses, ships rowing toward some distant shore.

There might as well have been mountains. Because what I did not know then—what I would learn only after his arrest—was that Kevin was experiencing symptoms of abrupt withdrawal from Sinequan, the antidepressant medication he'd been prescribed for over a year. He'd decided, some two weeks prior, that he didn't like how the pills made him feel, and so the bottle remained, unopened, in a drawer inside his desk.

But to abruptly discontinue from a high dose such as his meant nightmares, nausea, vomiting. It meant loss of coordination and dizziness, increased fatigue and severe depression. In the most extreme cases, I've learned, abrupt withdrawal from antidepressant medications—rather than a tempered, gradual reduction—can cause mania, suicidal ideation, even symptoms of psychosis.

I knew Kevin had suffered and perhaps continued to suffer from depression, and while it seemed likely he was on medication, I had no idea, that April night, just how bad my friend was feeling, though perhaps he didn't, either, until the moment that he killed Emily. What I knew then was only that we were about a month away from graduation. It was the Thursday before the long Easter weekend, and come morning, I planned to drive the three hours east to Telford to eat honeyed ham beside an artificial fireplace in my grandparents' over-fifty-five condo. I'd unwrap foiled chocolates tangled in plastic Easter grass, I thought, spoon homemade jam over cranberry bread. Without Friday classes, I could leave that very night if I wanted—arrive home in Telford to eat supper beside my parents or throw the dog's ball into the darkening yard. Instead, I stood on my fire escape in Gettysburg, watching the moon rise big and slow over Pennsylvania Hall and the darkening dorms. It was only three stories high, but that balcony offered the best view of Gettysburg: the downtown and flickering main street, the miles of untouched land, the observation towers rising up, giant pillars to support an electric sky. I watched taillights blink and brake, women jog by in thin, black nylon, living room lamps pop on from timers, their rooms suddenly alive with light.

There was another light that night, too—the shaky bulb from one man's lantern. He was leading a haunted ghost tour for out-of-towners from Cincinnati, maybe newlyweds from Poughkeepsie, children swinging bayonets at their fathers' ankles or clutching the loose fabric hanging off their mothers. He led them down our campus walkways, past one building and then another, all the while warning them to fear the many things they could sense but not yet see.

The embittered lover who haunted Glatfelter. The blue boy said to appear in windows outside Stevens Hall.

"The ghosts are all around us," he said, "watching everything we do." I knew this because I'd been on a similar tour, many years ago, as a child. In fact, my parents had been students at Gettysburg College as well, and met in October of 1976 at a party in honor of my father, whom my mother did not yet know. She knew only what one blond senior had told her as he threw a Frisbee across the darkening quad: that she was pretty, and she seemed fun, and she should come drink beer that night and dance. And that when she saw my father in his foyer's landing, he was wearing an orange windbreaker.

"It was a curious choice," she said, "but I liked it."

When we were children, my parents brought my brothers and me to Gettysburg each summer to tour the empty battlefields and moonlit walkways where they'd first fallen in love. *Retracing our roots*, my father called it, but mostly this meant packing brown-bag lunches filled with the food items we weren't normally allowed: Gushers and Doritos and Fruit Roll-Ups, Dunkaroos and Fruit by the Foot.

"This is a vacation," my mother would say, standing in the snack aisle of the grocery store, "so pick out what you think would be fun."

As a family, we'd pile into the big green minivan in what was the still-dark, still-quiet night, then drive the three hours west to Gettysburg to tour the battlefields in the early morning, while the sun was still low and cool. We'd spend our day in the downtown gift shops and the Gettysburg museum, watch as an animatronic Abraham Lincoln moved and spoke to us from behind thick glass, and our afternoons were spent in the motel pool, floating around on neon noodles.

But our nights were always reserved for campus: those lamp-lit sidewalks and dark, empty buildings. *This is where your father took class*, my mother would say, or *This is where we read*.

I was a legacy—a fact I would think about for days and months after it happened: how I was *born* because of Gettysburg, *raised* because of Gettysburg, *possible* because of Gettysburg—and yet it was that very place that I now feared would forever shape who I'd become.

He walked me home, and then he killed her.

Gettysburg was in my blood—more home to me than school—and so I knew when I enrolled I'd have to entertain the idea of ghosts. It was all anyone talked about those first few days—what if we saw one on a trip to the bathroom? What if we were accosted in the downstairs kitchen?

"They're not like vampires," someone said. "You can't just wave garlic in the air for protection."

Even the night of the First-Year Walk—the night I first met Kevin—it was as if I were trying to will them to appear. I was bored, hungry for action. I wanted to believe some legacy of those men lived on. I found myself staring up at the chapel's steeple, its small gray roof, its four stoic pillars.

Charming is what I thought, simply.

Years earlier, my parents had entertained the idea of marrying in that church, but settled instead for a small white chapel that always reminded me of a wedding cake in my mother's hometown in Massachusetts.

"Because the ghosts sort of freaked me out," she'd say, and I could never tell if she was kidding.

Beyond the church, Stevens Hall loomed big and white; it was allegedly the most haunted building on our campus, said to be possessed by the ghost of a small blue boy who appeared on the coldest nights in dorm room windows.

"It used to be an all-girls hall," a ghost-tour guide had told me once. I was six, or seven maybe, and leaned against my father, nervous, pressing my small body between his legs.

The ghost tour had been his idea—earlier, he'd asked my brothers and me if we were interested in learning the history we couldn't get from textbooks or by touring the battlefields, and yes, of course we were, because we were young and obsessed with death. We'd spent that day, in fact, standing idly above those fields while our parents stooped to read each placard, each text boxed around a grayscale image. They wanted to learn passively, from a distance, but we were imagining war, the violence unfolding all around us. We swung our toy bayonets purchased from the nearby gift shops and made fighting, struggling sounds.

"Hi-ya!" we said. "Hi-ya!"

The ghost tour seemed a good alternative—a quiet way to make his children care—and as I stood beneath my father that night outside of Stevens, I watched as he lowered the brim of his ball cap and squinted up into the setting sun. I followed his gaze upward, imagining a boy floating in the air by the roof.

"One night," the guide said, "some of the residents took in a runaway from the local orphanage on Baltimore Pike, and when the headmaster knocked on the door, they told him to hide on the window ledge. But by the time they returned an hour later, he was nowhere to be found. Now his face appears in bedroom windows on the coldest nights of winter."

I couldn't see him that night with my parents, and I couldn't see him the night of the First-Year Walk, either. I scanned each window individually, squinting, trying to make out his shape.

Come on, I thought, indignant, certain he would appear if I could only make it look as though I weren't watching. So I kicked pebbles into the street, trying to predict which stone would get hit first, and every now and then I'd glance up and over my classmates—over Kevin, in there, somewhere—to look up at the big, white building and search for the face of someone blue and lost.

Nearly four years later, as I stood on my fire escape that April night, I rolled my eyes at the guide's roaming lantern. I rolled my eyes at his haunted tour. It was easy, from that distance, to denounce something so obviously unbalanced and rooted in a need for deep significance.

Ghosts were something people *wanted* to believe in, I thought, so as to make the mundane feel inspired. Four years in Gettysburg, and I'd never seen a single ghost. I'd never heard a staircase creak or a hallway shift above the earth. I didn't understand then that ghosts were real—perhaps not in their embodiment, but in the way they could possess a mind.

The way one could remain haunted years after a death.

From my place along the fire escape, I told Kevin to lighten up. "Kevin," I said. "*Kevin*. How can you say no to an electric sky?"

And *fine*, he told me, *sure*, he couldn't see why not, and what was pink went blue, then black, as nightfall overtook our tiny town.

In the Blue Parrot Bistro an hour later, we chose the big, round table in the center of the room. I remember a cranberry tablecloth and a cluster of tea lights, Norah Jones sifting soft from the speakers mounted above, and that there were seven of us in all—friends who had been friends for years. Kevin wore a navy blue sweatshirt, which is what he wears in all my memories, and behind him hung the painting: a vibrant, neon bird, its head turned upright and alert.

Of everything in that room, it's the bird I remember best. I imagined hanging it above my fireplace in some distant, future home beneath potpourri and votive candles. That whole evening, in fact, as Kevin talked, I was looking not at him but at that painting—at the way the reds and greens and blues blended across the canvas, and how the bird's eyes were sharp and full of life, of what I imagined unsurpassable ambition. He was staring at something—something just out of focus, something emerging slowly, perhaps, from the brush somewhere behind him, and at some point in the night, I remember standing up to get a closer look, leaning in and inspecting the brushstrokes, running my finger over the smooth, clean canvas.

"This is fantastic," I said aloud.

"Are you listening?" Kevin asked.

It's the desire I remember now: how I wanted that painting more than anything, how it seemed a marker of a future life. Even now, despite every effort, I recall very little of Kevin's demeanor, or if his behavior was different in any way. If he was acting strangely—if he admitted any sadness to me at all— I have no way of knowing. I was imagining my children and how they'd hover beneath the painting, suggesting names to one another—*Henry*, or *Cookie*, or *Pepe*—because *of course* they'd give him a name.

From the front of the bar, a bell chimed, and Kevin walked me home.

"It's only a block," I said. "I can see my apartment building, even."

"Still," he said.

We reached the top step of my apartment building and then Kevin turned, so that the last image I have of him—before the orange jumpsuit, before his hands were cuffed and clasped around his waist—is of him retreating into the distance, his hair a brown mushroom cap, his hands stuffed inside his pockets. Later, I'd try to remember anything else—the expression he last gave to me, the way his T-shirt smelled—but all I remember now is how Kevin looked, heading away.

And I remember our graduation-gown fitting, some several months before Emily's murder: how, weeks earlier, I stood beside Kevin in the school gymnasium as women pinned fabric to our waists, our legs, our shoulders, squeezing our thickest parts, saying, *This fabric does not breathe.*

"You'll remember this day forever," they said, sewing pins pressed between their teeth, "and these gowns are a part of that memory."

Looking across at Kevin, swallowed whole in his long black robe, it wasn't difficult to imagine. I envisioned our robe-lined bodies stretching out across the makeshift stage, two of a steady thread of students, the sun shining white and hot as if to usher us into something new. It was almost too easy to imagine—this cliché of a defining moment, one we'd been waiting for forever. Every May for three long years, we'd walked past construction crews as they stacked clean, white chairs in careful rows, and now we'd sit among them. From our place in the audience, we'd be eye-level with the windows of those basement classrooms, the ones once used as makeshift hospitals, our seats along the grass the place where limbs had famously been piled. But for the seconds when we found ourselves onstage—as we reached out for those diplomas—our view would be of faces, the library, the winding pathways. The sparkling fountain and the flower beds and the dogwoods in rich, white bloom. We'd look out, in other words, and only see our pleasant future: all those sun-kissed buildings and subway cars, people pressing in between us in winter coats and knit-wool scarves.

Or maybe that's not what Kevin saw at all. Maybe standing there in that gymnasium during our gown fitting, people poking him from every side, Kevin only saw himself alone, solitary in some strange, new city. Maybe that morning the changes were only beginning inside his brain—synapses firing and then short-circuiting—or maybe that's not right, either.

Maybe that, too, was still weeks away.

Maybe all Kevin wanted in that moment was a slice of pizza and a Cherry Coke. There's no way for me to know. All I knew was that our futures were coming, big and bright as trains, like something you squint your eyes against in the enormity of it all. That day, during that fitting, our parents already had their dinner reservations, and hotel reservations, and my own mother had pulled me into the upstairs hallway to spin in the dress she planned to wear for the ceremony. She looked serene before her wall-length mirror.

"What do you think?" she asked softly, lowering her arms in her thin, black cotton tunic. The neckline was rimmed with golden stones so delicate they seemed dredged from an ocean floor.

"Beautiful," I said. "You'll look beautiful in that."

Later, on the downstairs porch, I sat beside my father as he pulled a Nikon Coolpix from its careful packaging. He leaned in low to show me: *Look at this optical zoom, look at this ten-second timer. Look—would you just look—at all of these special effects.*

"Twelve million pixels," he said, joking, "to capture *every* second."

There are remarkably few photographs of me taken on graduation day, but in every single one, I'm always posing with someone new—my mother, father, a roommate, my brother and his new wife—and in each, my eyes are scrunched, small, my smile forged as if in a foreign language. Scientists, I once read, can determine whether a smile is or is not genuine just by looking at photographs; it has to do with the tightening of facial muscles, the reflexive constricting of the forehead and jaw. But there's no need for complex research to understand my expression.

You can see it in my eyes.

In every photo, my smile is forced, my gaze fixated on someplace else. Like a block away from that grassy quad, where Emily had died on a bedroom rug. Or five miles away from that, where I presumed Kevin still sat in solitary confinement. Or farther, even still: to Oley, Pennsylvania, and two parents sitting on a couch, or sitting in a car, or sitting at a restaurant, because their son was not graduating and it no longer mattered where they were; they were not at the ceremony where they belonged.

"You did it," my mother said, squeezing my body into hers, and later—in a restaurant lit entirely by tea lights—we drank red wine and ate crème brûlée, the ramekins garnished with lemon peels, while in a cell just miles north, Kevin ate a grilled cheese sandwich, or an orange wedge, or a slice of lasagna, or maybe he ate nothing that night at all.

We had no idea what our futures held, and that's precisely what we talked about the night he killed her: how we were scared, no, *terrified*, because we had no idea what came next.

Life beyond Gettysburg had always been an abstraction—a complex notion of generalities with relatively few specifics—but now that it was a month away, we wanted answers to all our questions: Which city would we go to, and what would we do when we arrived? How would we afford it and who would we live with and how in the world would we meet anyone?

Everything was still so unknown, which we'd hoped would be exhilarating but seemed terrifying, and that's why Kevin had planned a trip—a drive across the country, he said, because everything else remained unclear.

"But this much," he said, "is certain, and it'll happen no matter what."

Kevin didn't yet have a job, and he was hesitant to begin graduate school right away, he said, because he didn't know what he wanted to do with his life, really, except he wanted it to be about music: promoting new bands and scheduling concerts, working with new artists and producing albums. So maybe he would head to Nashville, he said, or maybe New York City.

Los Angeles, too, sounded promising, and he had friends in San Francisco.

But in the meantime, with no offers available and nothing in the way of savings, what else could he do but reclaim his former bedroom in Oley, Pennsylvania, on the second floor beside the oak tree? Get a job at the public library? Maybe wait and see what happened?

"I can't afford anything else," he said. "I can't even count on minimum wage."

Kevin's relationship with his parents was not strained, but it was distant, the way it often is at twenty-two. We were still in that transitional phase between adolescence and adulthood, spending nine months of our year sifting cheap vodka through Brita filters four, five, six times to make it smooth. We smoked bubblegum hookah on rooftops and downed sake like it was water, the aftertaste burning in our throats, then cut across the campus to attend poetry readings by award-winning authors. The homes we'd be returning to in May had curfews, complaints about clothing, comments about our priorities and how we didn't think of them often enough.

"My house, my rules," my father would say, or "I want you home by eleven o'clock."

Telford and Oley were lovely places to visit: we ate our mothers' suppers and felt indulged by sweet white wine. But they were no place to return to.

And yet the economy was bad, it was so bad, and even now, all these years later, June of 2009 marks the highest unemployment rate in the ongoing economic crisis. Pennsylvania was ranked twenty-second at the time, which meant that it would be tougher in California, in New York, in Massachusetts. In

Florida or Illinois or Colorado or Washington, D.C. It would be tougher, even, in New Jersey. Compared with every other place we could want to go, Pennsylvania was doing, somehow, better.

"It all seems so impossible," Kevin said, shaking his head in that dimly lit bar.

And it was hard, that night, to argue. The only graduates we knew at the time still lived at home in their parents' basements, or they lived in cramped, one-bedroom apartments they shared with strangers they'd met on Craigslist. Patrick, a philosophy major who'd graduated the previous spring, lived ten miles away from Gettysburg in the only apartment he could afford: a brick, windowless structure butted up against the train tracks. He worked long hours as a waiter at a nearby Bennigan's and came home to microwavable entrées—mashed potatoes and fried chicken, frozen corn and lukewarm pudding—and it seemed a devastating divergence from the campus dining hall, our lemon-baked salmon, our spicy Thai noodles. Our gluten-free bread and our seitan and our tempeh. Some nights, he confided, he didn't even bother to spoon them out.

"Too tired, usually," he said, so he ate them from their plastic, those black cartons with pierced saran.

Each night, the trains blew past him at regular intervals—first at five, and then at seven, and then at nine and eleven and one—carrying coal or apples or who knows what, shuffling goods to better places. His plates and bowls and silverware rattled against the table as the trains blew past and blew their horns, but the vibrations, Patrick told us, were far worse than any whistle.

"They've knocked cups straight off the drying rack," he said. "I come home to broken glass."

We couldn't imagine a worse reality.

But it was only April, we told ourselves, and of course, we still had prospects: There was the Peace Corps or Teach for America. There were summer jobs, my friends admitted, places that might offer cheap employment.

"I can lifeguard until September," they said, or "I can babysit the neighborhood kids."

What was one more college graduate folding clothes at the local Hollister?

It was better than an unpaid internship, we agreed, which was the only other position anyone seemed capable of securing. Still, it was devastating: how hard we'd worked to polish our résumés for a forty-hour workweek in business slacks and button-downs while toting business cards, and that none of that would matter. People just weren't hiring.

So Kevin had planned a trip—it was a present to himself. On the morning following graduation, he'd cross the Mason-Dixon Line, just ten miles south of Gettysburg, then hug mountain overpasses of the Shenandoah before sweeping straight on through the Carolinas. At Atlanta, he'd head west. He'd keep going until he tired.

"Maybe I'll see the whole country," he said. "Elvis's grave, maybe camp out in Yellowstone."

He wanted to see Nashville, or maybe Tulsa.

He wanted to eat Southern barbecue and take a picture of the Badlands.

"It's going to be amazing," he said, "all of that red rock."

"It is," I said, "amazing," and then I joked how he would find himself: how on that open road after all those miles, Kevin would find himself anew. "A life-changing journey!" I said, laughing, and I began to sing John Denver's "Country Roads."

"I'll pass through most of them," Kevin said, "but I won't let them take me home."

The joke wasn't even funny—that's what gets me, even now: how we laughed like it was something special. How we had no idea it was our last.

That conversation—and that bad joke—was the final piece of dialogue Kevin and I would share outside of prison, and it's the worst thing worth remembering.

It's the absolute lousiest final memory.

Kevin told his joke and then he turned for home, but first I told him something: I'd been offered a job in Iowa, I said, fourteen hours from Pennsylvania.

"Teaching undergraduates," I said, "as part of graduate school admission."

Kevin had been with me when, months earlier, I'd first made the decision to apply, citing a need for an advanced degree.

"I'm a Writing Across the Genres major with an emphasis in poetry," I'd joked. "No one's going to hire me without a master's. *I* wouldn't hire me."

I'd applied to fifteen schools in all, all of them out of state.

"I'm fucked if I don't get in," I'd said. "I'm literally screwed if it doesn't work out."

"You'll be fine," Kevin had said, nodding. "You're a shoo-in. You'll get in."

It was my acceptance, in fact, we were celebrating when I'd called, hours earlier, on that condemned and rusting fire escape. I wanted, I'd said, to celebrate. I'd been packing for Easter weekend—folding jeans and selecting tank tops—when I received a call from a program director, inviting me to join him.

"You'll even design a class," he'd said, "design your own syllabus, create assignments."

Iowa was a place of corn and farmland, not altogether different from Pennsylvania, but still it meant a departure: from Gettysburg, from Telford, from the dusty riverbed trailer parks and one-lane bridges and gravel dead-end drives. I imagined fields of yellow that stretched outward, tall, thin strands of wheat, women wearing denim overalls and wide-brimmed hats in prairie grass. In Iowa, I learned, even time would be different.

There'll be complications phoning home, I thought, though of course this wasn't true.

I imagined the desolate, heartbreaking landscapes and how I'd shape them into something beautiful.

Pennsylvania was gorgeous but it was lonely, I'd write, and later, in a bar with my new friends, I'd say, "I got out of there just in time."

The university where I'd soon teach was home to

thirty thousand students—twenty-eight thousand more than Gettysburg—and I pictured the bookstores and record shops, the Indian and Thai and Vietnamese restaurants I hoped I might find. Iowa City offered public pools and public parks and a complicated grid of public transportation, and on a schedule I found online, I sat transfixed by the colorful labyrinth, which seemed indicative of a foreign elegance, the way the lines bent and converged, veering beautifully across the map.

The suburbs surrounding my new campus offered not one but two gigantic malls, I learned, plus a Best Buy and a Bennigan's, an Olive Garden and an Applebee's. I'd have a Sears and Younkers and Macy's, and both a Starbucks and a Caribou Coffee, and I imagined visiting them both—buying an iced latte from one vendor and a snowflake cookie from the other, just because I could. I'd be overwhelmed by all my options. And later, in a small lot beside the mall, I'd visit a place called HuHot that offered, "Create your own Asian stir fry."

My new life would begin in August, just three months after graduation.

"My friend, the budding professor," Kevin said, standing beside me on that sidewalk. "I'm really happy for you." And why didn't I tell him sooner, he asked, if I'd been with him all night long?

"I didn't want to discourage you," I said. "I know you'll find something soon."

Kevin looked at me and blinked, and I recognized first confusion and then something else. Later, I'd try to read into it—the curved lines around his mouth, the way his eyes shot downward—and think, *He clearly felt overwhelmed.* I'd think, *This is all my fault.*

But in reality, Kevin was likely just putting the pieces together. How all night I'd sat quietly at our table, pretending to listen, but in my head I'd been making plans: thinking shades of paint and throw rugs, imagining the color I'd paint my headboard.

Cream, I'd decided, gender-neutral, invoking maturity, intellect.

I'll cook fancy meals, I'd thought, *for friends I'll meet in the teachers' lounge.* We'd share wide, flat Italian noodles and grade papers at my kitchen table.

"Are you scared?" Kevin asked. "I mean, it's a lot of change at once."

"No," I said, "I'm not," but it was a lie and we both knew it.

"Well," he said. He scuffed his shoe along the curb. "I'm really proud of you."

And that's when I said it, not knowing what else to say. I said, "Don't you worry." I said, "You always have that drive."

"Sure," he said, nodding. "And all those country roads."

I was drunk and I was tired and I didn't think any more about it; I'd found my way out of Pennsylvania, and I didn't think it was that big a deal that he hadn't yet. In retrospect, perhaps Kevin was intimidated by the change, of being alone in the familiar, but I, too, was afraid—being alone in Iowa, in the vast and deep unfamiliar, seemed even scarier still. And regardless, he would get to see those roads. He would eat pulled pork beside a highway stand. Maybe this, in fact, is what he was thinking about, hours later, as he sat beside her: how he'd never get to see anything, how he had murdered a young woman. How nothing else could ever matter because he'd ended someone's life.

I know now from the written testimony by not one but three mental health professionals that Kevin was likely unable to distinguish right from wrong in the moment that he killed her, or at least unable to act upon that notion, but not in the immediate aftermath; in those first few minutes after, he took panicked steps to revive her, first tying her pants around her neck in an attempt to alleviate blood loss, then carrying her to the tub when he knew that wouldn't work. He sat beside her body for "twenty to forty minutes," according to the paperwork, trying to determine what had happened, likely grieving her life in absence, while a block away, I got up for a glass of water, thought about my office, my future students and their thoughtful questions. The blazers I would wear. My hair secured with pencils.

It's likely because of my own inebriation that Kevin finally called Claire, who lived in a house two blocks away. Claire was Emily's best friend, and perhaps this is why Kevin called her, or perhaps Kevin called Claire because he knew I was too drunk to take that call. I would've slept right through it, or else I would've picked it up and said, *What the hell, you jerk?*

"It's four o'clock in the goddamn morning," I'd say, even before he had the chance to speak. "What's your fucking problem?" And I would think he was being funny: prank calling, asking for Professor Butcher. Saying, *Are you available for office hours?*

The point, however, is that Kevin called Claire, and when she saw Emily's body—the outline of limbs hugged tight by a shower curtain—she told him what they had to do: They had to phone the police, she said. They had to make this right.

Kevin promised to surrender himself immediately, but first wanted to call his parents to say good-bye. "I've done an awful thing," he said. "Emily," he said.

From their still-dark home in Oley, Mr. and Mrs. Schaeffer told their only son to call the police, that they were on their way, and then they clicked on a bedside light and pulled on first jeans and then socks and then sneakers. They started their car, backed out of the drive, and began the two-hour trip to Gettysburg, where their son sat silent beside Claire as she dialed 911.

"There's been a terrible thing," she said, and then Kevin excused himself to wait on the sidewalk outside his home, his hands clasped behind his head as if already a part of his future self.

My glass empty, my throat parched, I got back in bed, and I might've been dreaming about the ocean as police officers lowered him into their car. Maybe squids or undercurrents or the way mountains can rise from nearly nothing and in their landscape become everything. And while I could later imagine the police cruiser driving first down Washington Street and then Lincoln Avenue—see the early-morning commuters

click on their turn signals and pull over along the shoulder—
I didn't actually see that car or its kaleidoscope of color.

I didn't hear the noise.

I slept soundly, and that cruiser continued moving, quickly traversing the space between us, and then the whole morning was quiet, and my friend Kevin stopped waiting.

6

ALTHOUGH I WISH I could say otherwise, there was no sequential separation distancing Kevin's violent actions from my instinctual urge to comfort him. My response was compassion and it was prompt. In fact, the chief emotion I experienced during those first few hours was not grief or fear at all—though those would present themselves shortly thereafter and with unparalleled intensity—but absolute resolution: I would help him through this moment. And because to help, I thought, meant to learn, I found myself quickly obsessed with what had happened.

This was due, in part, to youthful naiveté—a rubberneck sensation caused by knowing a murder beyond TV—but the larger part, I now suspect, was due to the crime's grotesque violence and how unprecedented that act had been: *27 times, 27 times, 27 times.* It was a detail every newspaper article included, because it was the detail that meant *horrendous.* It was a detail that implied psychotic, blinding, or sudden rage. Kevin was a monster, in other words; there was no other way around what he had done. His actions unearthed many questions— *Why was Emily at his apartment at four o'clock in the morning? And was this something he'd intended? Could this have been* planned *in any way?*—but what was clear and without question was how many times he stabbed Emily Silverstein in the shallows of her neck, just beneath her collarbone, and across her throat.

Kevin, who liked Twizzlers and pizza and the Civil War and history. Kevin, who once lent me his sneakers because my sandals were giving me blisters—"I'll go barefoot," he'd said. "It's no problem"—and later, when I offered to wash them, he rolled his eyes and said, "Are you kidding?"

Kevin—who wore bright green sneakers—had stabbed that woman twenty-seven times.

I had no experience with anything so sensational; violence had no place yet in my world. At twenty-two, the most traumatic event I'd ever endured was attending my grandmother's funeral, but even then, she'd been sick and suffering. I'd left flowers beside her grave and thought, *It's better now that she's gone.*

I knew that sometimes, for no real reason, bad things happened to good people, but I also believed—in earnest—that these people would never be people I knew. I didn't understand yet, because I didn't know to, that lives could get interrupted, that in no way was an existence like a train lumbering along a track; a life could swerve or dislocate. An existence could stop or even crash. From an early age, I'd been taught to be polite, and taught to be bilingual, and taught to know exactly where to place the fork and the spoon and the knife in the delicate setting of a dinner table, and somehow I always assumed this would enable me to avoid the pain and suffering I could identify but not alleviate in others.

This was just one of many things I believed before Kevin's crime: that somehow a person could absolve herself from the world's misery simply by being intelligent, or courteous, or careful. By donating money to endangered wildlife or volunteering time at an animal shelter.

I thought, *My life has—and always will be—beautifully blessed.*

At times, I want to hate the person I used to be, but it was all I'd ever known. My parents had raised my brothers and me in a quiet Mennonite town where everyone knew everyone, or we knew everyone by association. As children, we gave brooches of birds or stargazer lilies to our bus drivers every June.

"For getting you home safely," my mother would say, tucking the gift inside my tiny fist. "You look her in the eyes when you give her this."

My mother was a French teacher, and my father was a chemist who designed vaccines for incurable illnesses. One summer, when his research team created a cure for hepatitis C, they threw a party in our backyard, *and there were ponies*, I told everyone. *We even rented ponies!*

There was a vanilla sheet cake that read *Congratulations on Hep-C!* in rich, white buttercream, and I spent the day beside the pool, sipping SunnyD and eating Cheetos, sunning myself on a neon towel atop the hazy, too-hot concrete.

Even the home where I'd been raised—even *that* was sheltered from all that was sad and ugly. Our house was two stories of brick set atop a hillside in the middle of the Pennsylvania countryside. We were an anomaly. We were surrounded by decaying structures, collapsed bridges, creeks filled with empty Coke cans gone orange from neglect and time, but I never knew that hardship—neither wanting nor desperation. Our trespassers were deer. Our front door was always unlocked.

All I knew of tragedy, in fact, was what I'd gleaned from current events: a plane crashes into towers, or a bomb ignites and implodes a building. An earthquake shakes the ground, tremors seizing land in bursts for days.

A tsunami crashes into a coastline.

A tornado makes the sky go green.

But the news the morning after came via a small, pixelated envelope that appeared in my inbox between an email from my mother and one from Bed Bath & Beyond.

A student has been fatally stabbed, it read, though it said nothing of that student's identity or the identity of the person—or student—who had stabbed him or her.

I tried but could not imagine what had happened in our small town. I pictured a boy from my biology class, then his lanky body in a gutter. I pictured the girl who worked the mailroom, then her pleated skirt along a sidewalk. There was the chalk outline of a figure, the long, thin shape of a stretcher, men in black hats and overcoats lifting a body from a curb.

But none of it fit the Gettysburg I knew, where the violence was always scripted and the blood always imagined. So it was a burglary gone wrong, I decided. Or two fraternity brothers, drunk and jousting.

What seemed certain, most of all, was that I couldn't have

known the two involved. This is where the mind goes: You think, *Something this awful doesn't happen to me.* What I thought and never questioned was that someone else would get that news; someone else would get that call.

A mother in southern New Jersey, some father in the suburbs of Hartford.

My friends were vegetarians or they were Democrats or they didn't spend seventy-five dollars on a Ralph Lauren button-down. They were celebrating Easter on campus that weekend because they valued what little time they had left with one another before graduation, or because they were international students from Nepal, or because they couldn't afford to fly home because they were paying their own way through college. My friends were members of Amnesty International and they went hiking and grew their own basil. They weren't the type to murder.

In the parking lot beside my apartment, I loaded my bags into my trunk. I decided I'd drive home, where I'd eat carrot cake with my family, and my friends would call me from Gettysburg to share the news as it unfolded. From the privacy of my childhood bedroom, I'd learn exactly what had happened.

Gettysburg stabbing, I'd type into Google. *Homicide*, I'd write.

But while idling at a red light just off campus, I noticed the yellow tape stretching across Carlisle Street and, beyond it, in a yard, the shadows of men clustered around a mailbox. It was a house I knew well, because it was the one where Kevin lived.

It was the one, too, where Andrew, and Helen, and Beth lived—the four had rented that home so that they might burn incense and throw backyard barbecues, let everything hang heavy with the scent of charcoal and rich patchouli. But they rented it, too, because it was perfect: split-level with four bedrooms and butted right up against the battlefields. Andrew and Helen occupied the two ground-level apartments, and Kevin and Beth shared the upstairs, the door linking the two floors bolted shut to ensure privacy.

"It's weird," I said when I first noticed it, a week after Kevin moved in. He'd invited us over for an impromptu happy hour, and stood in the kitchen, slicing lemons.

"It's annoying when we want to have parties," he said, "but it's no big deal to just go around the side."

Later, in his bedroom, he pulled back the curtains to reveal his inspiring view. "Amazing, huh?" he asked us, nodding out at the open fields. "There's nothing out there for miles."

Now I sat silent in my car, studying the fluorescent tape. I reached for my phone and listened as it rang once, twice, three times before it went to voicemail.

"Hi, it's Kevin," the voice said. "And I'm not here right now."

"It's me," I said. "Just want to make sure you're okay."

Classes hadn't been canceled, so I decided he must be in one. I pictured his thin frame hunched over a desk, his head turned toward a window where, blocks south, detectives were combing through his living room, taking fibers from his floors. I imagined his concern, the careful weight nestled in his stomach. *What it must feel like*, I thought, *to have people going through your things.*

But at a rest stop an hour later—when he still hadn't returned my call, even though all courses had since let out—I called our shared friend Leslie, who said he hadn't been to class in the first place.

"He didn't come to class," she said, "and we've heard from all of them but him."

What she meant was Andrew, Helen, and Beth. Everyone else who lived in Kevin's house was accounted for except him. Beth had left earlier in the week to visit family, Leslie said, and Andrew and Helen had been spotted whispering in a back booth of the cafeteria, but neither one would reveal just what they knew.

"Leslie," I said. "Where's Kevin?"

She was silent for a moment—a hesitation I indulged briefly as the by-product of seeing him making his way toward her, a backpack over his shoulder, an excuse that he'd cut class. He wanted to see the battlefields in golden sunlight, or eat a slice of cake at the Lincoln Diner.

But it was interrupted by her words: "I don't know, Amy. I don't know."

Worse yet was what we could not, in that moment, even begin to think to fathom: that a thorough answer—the *why*, if not the *how*—would come not in days, not in weeks, not in months. Not for nearly two years, when I'd finally drive to the courthouse in Gettysburg and sit in a hard, red plastic chair, the kind I'd used in kindergarten, and say, "I'm here to see some court documents. I'm here to see what's public record."

We don't gather around a burning building to help, William Hazlitt writes in his 1826 essay "On the Pleasure of Hating."

We gather to watch it burn, and in the weeks following Kevin's incarceration, that's what everyone I knew—and did not know—did.

It was easy to do exactly that because of the Internet, which provided a public and anonymous space. Of the many news agencies carrying Kevin's story, not one required their users to register. There were no moderators or censors or warnings, no polite requests urging sensitivity. So here is where the spectators gathered, warming their hands above a still-burning fire.

I hope he's gang raped in prison for the next 50 years, wrote one man on NJ.com. *Let's not sugarcoat this story: Kevin Schaeffer's an animal.*

I agree, wrote Hve20, *assuming the state doesn't have the death penalty, 50 years of prison gang rape sounds about right for this guy.*

At the *Reading Eagle*, a user named Missing wrote, *An eye for an eye—am I right?*

Over on PennLive.com, on an article announcing Kevin's guilty plea, users took a different approach, commenting not on what Kevin deserved, but on the causation for Emily's death. *What I want to know*, wrote Mr.Youlookdumberthanyouthink, *is what was a Jewish girl doing with a German-American boy? That is the only valid question; this could have all been avoided.*

Two words, wrote a user named Rick, *"death penalty."*

Two hours later, he commented again. *Two words*, he repeated, *"death penalty."*

Users were angry about Kevin's crime, or they were angry about his past. They questioned his identity and future and the presumed outcome of his criminal trial. Because Kevin had admitted to police that he'd recently weaned himself off

Sinequan, citing he didn't "like how the drugs [made him] feel," users slammed the idea of chemical imbalance, arguing, *This was murder, plain and simple.*

I didn't bother to leave a comment. I didn't see the point. I read the comments only ever picturing Emily's parents, or Kevin's, saw them leaning into their computer screens, adjusting the light or their reading glasses. Certainly if I was Googling Kevin, or Emily, their parents were as well. And what good could ever come of it—from my comments, their comments, anyone's?

So writing Kevin directly seemed only natural. He was not a fire that I'd watch burn. The problem was not coming up with the words, as I'd expected, but finding a way to get my message out. It was the day before Easter, one day after his arrest, and I stood beside my mother as she sprinkled miniature marshmallows and brown sugar over a casserole of warm mashed yams.

"I'd prefer you not write him from here," she said, wiping her hands against her apron. "It's not that I think he'll get out," she said, "or even that he'd hurt you. I worry, mostly, about our privacy."

What she meant was our house: the two stories of brick on four undisturbed acres. Her implication was that this place was sacred, *safe*, and should not be made available to an inmate. That it was not something to be arranged and put down so specifically as a series of numbers and letters, a scribble that could later be hung on a jail cell inside a prison.

Telford was not—my mother implied—a place where Kevin should be able to reach me.

"You do what you need to do," she said, lowering the dish into the oven. "But this place is not for him."

The fact that I would write him, however, was never called into question, because as a teenager I'd crafted careful, detailed statements to parents and victims of national tragedies: first the parents of Matthew Shepard, the Wyoming gay youth left to die beside a fence post just outside of Laramie, then the mother of Cassie Bernall, killed in the Columbine massacre, because allegedly—in the final moments before her death— Cassie was asked if she believed in God, and when she told shooters Eric Harris and Dylan Klebold that yes, of course she did, they pressed the gun to her head and fired.

I'm so sorry about your loss, I wrote, and weeks later, when I received a response from her mother—*Thank you so very much*— I pinned it to my bedroom wall as an achievement.

I saw it as my duty: giving support to those who lacked it. For years, I awoke early to watch the news beside my parents, always waiting for the people I believed needed me the most. These were people who'd been scammed, hurt, scared, pushed onto train tracks in downtown Philadelphia or wounded in a drive-by shooting. I'd been raised with comfort and thought that what this meant was I should give it back to others. Securing their address was always easy: I'd send a letter to the news channel, or the organization founded in the child's name, and when the recipients wrote back, it was as if they'd been waiting for me all along.

We were so relieved to receive your letter, they'd write, or *You've made his memory come alive.*

So who but me would take care of Kevin in the aftermath

of what he'd done? The way one imagines the life of the driver being medevaced from the car accident—the children awaiting his return at home, the macaroni art taped to the refrigerator—the rubbernecking was relentless and it was thorough. I pictured Kevin in his jail cell, water dripping from a ceiling tile as a venting grate blew hot steam. This was the only image I had of prison, though it was not, I knew, the sort of facility Kevin was in. The Adams County Correctional Center was new, modern, clean, and I knew this because we'd passed it often on our way out of town to the neighboring thrift store. It was a monthly Saturday tradition: Eric, George, Kevin, and I piling into Keith's backseat and driving the thirty minutes east to buy vinyl records and old Coke bottles. We'd spend hours wandering the aisles, talking to elderly men about their collections—figurines or baseball cards—and on the way home, we'd pass the old prison, which had been used since the Civil War. It was located just beside the new one.

I pictured Kevin's face—once indicative of familiarity, it had since been replaced by the image broadcast the night before on the evening news, which made tangible the things he'd done. Before the television networks were able to get their hands on his booking photos, they'd used the image pulled directly from his student ID, which he used to buy sodas and books and candy, sandwiches, packs of gum. By evening, however, no longer was Kevin in his green T-shirt, smiling sheepishly at the camera; now he wore an orange jumpsuit, his eyes so strained and swollen they looked the deepest shade of purple.

"Jesus," I'd said aloud, sitting back against the couch.

Gettysburg had made Kevin highly educated and cultured and curious; he'd enrolled in courses on Buddhism and studied writing, read Hemingway and Camus and Proust. He looked you in the eye each time he spoke, and he talked of places he wanted to go, the types of people he hoped to find there, and while these had been desirable qualities at Gettysburg—evidence of careful grooming and strong parenting—in jail, they made him a target. I worried about the people in there with him—petty vandals, cocaine dealers—though Kevin would later tell me these were the types of people you *wanted* to be around. What was worse, he told me once, were the people just like him: murderers, rapists, pedophiles.

It seems smart to start bulking up, he wrote, and that was all he had to say.

Murder or no murder, I knew Kevin was experiencing things drastically different from anything I knew or could relate to, so I wrote him first out of obligation, or I wrote to him because I was curious. Maybe I wrote to him because I wanted to feel like a better friend—at this point, I can't honestly say. For so long, my motive didn't matter; I had a friend who was now in prison, and it was my job, I believed, to distract him from what he was experiencing while he was there.

I can't understand what you did, I wrote, then deleted it and began again. *I will try to understand*, I wrote, *but I wish this hadn't happened.*

It was all I could say—the only thing I knew with absolute certainty I'd never regret. Even then, I knew that details could emerge before Kevin received my letter, and so to say that I'd always be there for him, or that I would see this through, or that I trusted it was an accident—there seemed a risk in each admission.

I miss you, I wrote, and then I printed and folded the letter.

It took twenty minutes to get to the nearest grocery store, the only place I knew with certainty that had a mailbox along its exterior. It was a small-town place, the kind to give free slices of cheese to children as their mothers waited in the deli line, and as a child, I had stood often in that doorway, picking pumpkins as big as my head from a crate beside an ATM. I stood now beside a potted tree adorned with colorful plastic eggs, and when I finally reached that mailbox, I dropped the envelope inside.

It's just like writing a soldier, I thought on my long drive home, though of course this wasn't true. Still, I let myself see the parallel: Kevin was a man in a strange, foreign land, exploring a harsh and lonely landscape, and I was the woman who served as comfort—who wrote him with the hope that he wouldn't forget himself or who he was—or had been—to me.

It's just like that, I thought, knowing all the while that it was different.

There are other things I should admit, like how in my earliest childhood memory, I'm sitting beside my mother in our carpeted den in darkness, and I am rapt—absolutely rapt—as I wait for the impending violence. My mother has drawn the heavy shades and sits now with her feet tucked up beneath her, her simple daytime slippers made of satin and terry cloth, and through the television's blue static glow, I watch as her fingers angle and bend, her wrist elegant and thin as she presses buttons on a remote. I am five, or six maybe, and this is our hour independent of everyone else: my older brother Wesley still at school, my younger brother William asleep upstairs, my father mixing chemicals in a lab coat in the next town over.

"It's just us girls," my mother says, and in the kitchen, she pours what is left of the morning's coffeepot into a thermos. I add sugar—first one spoonful and then another—and then another, until finally the beverage is creamy and cool and sweet.

"Juuuuuust right," I say, as if I am Goldilocks, edging my toes across the linoleum, careful not to spill. Back in the den, we take seats on the sofa and the television screen startles into picture. Here is the show we love more than any other: a program where men kill women, or women kill men, or a body is found along a riverbed. A child disappears from a backyard swing set. A mother never arrives to a family picnic.

From beneath a floral bedspread, a woman dials 911.

"875 Parkhill Ridge," she says, or "23 Mulholland," or "8 Lakeview Vista." The address is never important; what matters, instead, is the way the woman says it: her voice muted and clipped, and how—almost immediately—a foot appears. There is someone else in this room, and he has heard her, and here's his shoe.

By the time the police arrive, the woman is nothing but a heavy stain, a rug missing from a living room parlor.

"If you have any information," the narrator says, and then my mother pulls back the curtains to reveal white daylight and sunlit pine. I stand beside her in our country kitchen as she slices Granny Smith apples into crescent moons, logs of cheese into bite-size portions. We sit together on the porch outside to wait for Wesley's school bus to chug up the road, kicking up dust and gravel, the family guinea pig chirping in my lap, the baby monitor on the windowsill: my brother's heavy sounds of sleep.

For years, this is how we lived: a morning of quiet work— my mother tidying while I played—and then an hour's worth of violence. We loved *Unsolved Mysteries* in a way I could never place; I liked the thrill of it, the way the show—coupled with coffee—felt off-limits and indulgent, but I liked it, too, for its threat of unprecedented danger within our quiet, suburban town. My mother was young, loved, and pretty, and though it'd take years for me to realize, that show—and the violence inherent to its every episode—was something she may well have needed: an hour of unthinkable brutality to remind her of the solace of a quiet home. Housework could be tedious and lonely, but my father's love was never a question.

And from a young age, I learned this: *The combination of these two realities is normal. Life is all of this at once.* It was both the woman folding tablecloths beside the antique cabinet, and then the woman's body later wrapped up in them.

But when I replay these memories to my mother now, she only laughs and shakes her head. "I shouldn't have let you watch that," she says, "but I was young, what did I know?"

Still, it was never the crimes that scared me. I remind her I never had nightmares.

"If you ever did, we would have stopped," she says. "I'm certain of that much."

But I never had them—deranged dreams, night sweats. What haunted me most never came in sleep. I wasn't frightened by the murders or kidnappings, not the cars squealing down dusty roads. It wasn't the man still on the loose, not the van with stolen tags. I understood, even at that young age, that those were dramatizations; those were character actors. Those were overly sensationalized dialogues and fictionalized landscapes and scripted phone calls. The men, in all likelihood, were very far away from us—in a desert somewhere in Utah, or a swampy marsh in Louisiana. They had no business in our rural Pennsylvania town, between the Poconos and Alleghenies, where mountain peaks rose and fell and you felt protected by their closeness.

I wasn't scared by the truth the show depicted, but by what they chose not to depict at all: How a man could be first your boyfriend, and then your husband, and then your cause of death. How he could drive himself to the local Kmart, buy a gun, and fill it with bullets.

Put your body in a river.

Put your body in a ditch.

So it wasn't nightmares that terrified me, but instead those moments of perfect clarity that always came just before sleep. It was always the general essence of a mind that I tried to picture, lying atop a comforter lined with the perfect faces of smiling snowmen. I imagined first the fibrous canals inside the brain, then how they lit and pulsated with color. These, which caused a man you loved to snap and snap your neck. These, which had the potential to make a man so angry he slit your throat, dumped you in a cornfield.

This was always what seemed to me the far greater, more pressing danger: what the mind was somehow doing when we weren't aware that it was doing it.

Back on campus the following Monday, it was as if another war had taken place, this one fresher and far more invisible without the fanfare of exploding cannons. Those of us who'd known Kevin felt like lepers, responsible by association. Each night, after classes and work and the things that kept us from one another, we gathered in a cramped apartment to spoon greasy food onto paper plates: lasagna or baked ziti, baked chicken breasts, spaghetti—whatever someone had found the time or the energy to make—and we served it from cheap aluminum we could dispose of when the night was through.

Those first few days, it was like a video game: as if in finding a hidden scroll, we could undo everything that had happened. As if in determining a magic code, we could bring Emily back to life.

It just doesn't make sense, we said again and again. There had to be something—some piece of the puzzle that was missing, some critical piece of understanding that would make everything else make sense. We didn't know yet that there was no one piece; there would be no making sense, because none could be made. Still, I'd listen each morning for the sound of the mailman's boots as they scuffed across the linoleum, his keys jingling against the door, and I'd prepare myself for the letter I was certain would eventually come: Kevin's perfectly detailed document, which would make sense of all that happened.

In the lobby, I'd sift through piles, shuffle coupons against catalogues, but it was only ever ads I held.

The following Thursday, the college held a memorial service for Emily in Christ Chapel in the heart of campus. I was working that afternoon in an office across the street, and I watched as students arrived in their pastel galoshes and black pantsuits, yellow rain jackets over dresses. I was excused from my afternoon duties, my supervisor had told me, *of course*, but I stayed at my tiny desk, uncertain what it was, exactly, that I should do. The sky over Gettysburg was dark, and the cameramen who lined the sidewalks propped their heavy umbrellas over equipment in anticipation of the gray sky and all its rain.

Everyone was there; they packed our small Lutheran church. But my grief was such that I hadn't yet even begun to mourn for Emily. I didn't think that I could focus on her death because it meant focusing on the person who had caused it. I felt sick, sad, alone—heartbroken for Emily and her family, but devastated, as well, for Kevin: for the life he'd lost that night. For his parents, two people in their fifties who'd lost their only son.

Now there would be no summer barbecues for the Schaeffers. No watermelon, no grilled chicken. There would be no grandchildren or alphabet place mats, no Goldfish crackers packed in neon plastic. The most recent photograph they had of their son, in fact, was the one broadcast on the evening news—his thin frame elongated in an orange jumpsuit, that image transmitted to thousands.

This was true for Emily's parents, too, of course, but I felt unable to even process that pain. Her face was everywhere—taped to trees outside her apartment, on the Facebook pages of everyone I knew or did not know—and in them, she was smiling, wearing green, pursing her lips. Her face was always cherubic; her expressions and gestures were full of life. She was the iconic symbol of tragic and premature death—beautifully innocent even in her accessories: holding an ice-cream cone, wearing hot-pink heart-shaped glasses.

And yet the very idea of attending her memorial seemed nothing if not selfish. I was not yet ready to parse that loss, and couldn't guarantee that, once inside her service, my thoughts would remain with Emily, in my processing of her death. To worry for Kevin while in my apartment seemed one thing, but to mourn the loss of his life at a ceremony that was meant to honor Emily's seemed another altogether.

Her parents would be there, I knew. Her brother and all her friends.

"You owe it to her to go," a friend had told me earlier that morning. "We can show up together if you want, but I really think you ought to go."

Instead I watched from my tiny office as students arrived

together, their arms linked, holding hands. I was the only one on campus, it seemed, who wouldn't be in attendance. So five minutes before it began, I walked across the street and entered the quiet church. Students had filled the aisles and entrance-ways and spilled out into the lobby, and I climbed the staircase to the upper level, found an empty spot, and took a seat. It was closest to the aisle; I could leave if I had to. But as the organ began to quiet, a woman squeezed in beside me.

"You don't mind?" she said. "Thanks."

Outside, I knew, the cameras were rolling, and if I had to leave—if all of this proved too much—their equipment would capture my retreat. My figure, slipping out of the service before it'd even begun: It could be broadcast to thousands.

"Excuse me," I said to the woman. "Excuse me, excuse me."

I pushed past her and through the chapel doors. I pushed past the cameramen and their bulky, black equipment. I walked fast, the campus diluting behind me.

In my apartment, I peeled off my jacket and boots and piled into bed with my wet hair, wet skin, wet clothes. I stared at Emily's face on the front of the service's handout. I sat study-ing her face, my own private memorial.

"I'm sorry," I said aloud. "I had no idea that this would happen."

If I had, I would have stopped it. I would have taken him to another bar. I would have taken him to another city. I would have dragged him into Maryland, said, "Let's go camp-ing," said, "Let's take a hike." In the middle of Virginia, we'd cook bacon in a pan till sunrise, and there'd be no time to meet with Emily, no need for a memorial at all.

• • •

It took Kevin four weeks to respond to my letter, and when he finally did, he didn't have much to say. *I can't talk about it*, he wrote, *because they monitor what I write. And I'm sorry I couldn't reply sooner, but I hope you understand the procedures I must go through.*

I have to fill out a request, he wrote, *just to clip my own fingernails.*

He was also blind, I learned. Because Kevin was what the prison system considered a "high-risk inmate," he had not yet been granted clearance to wear his glasses, on account of what he—or anyone—could do with them.

Right now, they have me in an isolation cell, he wrote, *on suicide watch. I can't see, so I can't read. The library has only two books printed in the bigger font, and I've read them both twice already.*

I learned, too, that Kevin was alone for twenty-three hours of every day. Save for the hour he was allowed outside in the empty courtyard—a basketball court and a picnic table—he spent his days in a six-by-four-foot cell in the facility's most private wing.

But I can hear everything that goes on next door, he wrote, *as if there aren't even concrete walls between us. One man is Muslim, and he prays aloud throughout the day. He sings it, too*, he wrote, *and it's a truly beautiful sound. He told me the Koran was meant to be sung and not said, Amy—did you know that?*

I didn't. I lowered his letter.

I imagined him folded into an empty corner of a hollow

jail cell, his elbows propped against his knees, his eyesight fuzzing the things he knew. He was blind and cold and alone, without books or even vision, but in the distance, someone was singing.

And what a beautiful, calming noise in a world of violent men.

My hope had always been that when finally I moved to Iowa, I would find the distance necessary to leave Kevin behind—not send him my new address, not tell him how to reach me.

Don't worry about losing your PA roots, he'd written. *You'll always have me here!*

And yet I did not want to have him. Nightmares seized me from sleep and I worried silently about unraveling—about what I was beginning to understand and refer to as a trauma. Everyone else around me, it seemed, had moved on and forgotten about Kevin. And I wanted—however cruelly—to forget about him, too.

But I didn't know what had happened—what had turned inside his brain and likely could turn inside mine, as well. That's what it came down to: how I simply didn't know. So the morning of my departure, I tore a sheet from an empty notebook.

You can find me here, I wrote, and then I drew a moving van and its heavy fumes as it startled into motion.

Already my car was packed full with lamps and a microwave and a smudged, full-length mirror, but I drove through the Pennsylvania countryside regardless, over back roads rutted with potholes and patches of shade from thick, dense trees. I stood again before the grocery store's mailbox, the heat radiating off the parking lot's pavement, blurring the farm and the open fields. I said good-bye to Pennsylvania and dropped my envelope inside.

7

I DON'T LIKE DESCRIBING what Kevin's actions began to do to me—and indirectly to those around me—without first saying that I was in love the night it happened, and that I trusted my boyfriend Keith, and that I respected him, that he made me feel safe. That what we had—what Keith offered—was not something I gave up easily. That he cooked me eggs in the shape of hearts and shoveled snow from the roof of my car. And that while his childhood had been difficult, he found in me a refuge; I was the person, he told me often, who had saved him from himself.

It's small and insubstantial in comparison, I realize: this abrupt end of a college relationship. But that's precisely the problem I face; I have a difficult time, even now, separating what is and is not connected.

Had it not been for what Kevin did, I think, *Keith and I might still be together.* And who knows what that future held, or how much more I'd likely prefer it.

Even when I first met Keith, the first month of freshman year, I knew that I was lucky. Keith was the sort of person I always envisioned as an integral part of my future life: he was smart, cute, and articulate, with a penchant for oatmeal half-zip sweaters and an interest in international travel. In fact it was this, more than anything, that drew me to him initially: He'd spent the last year backpacking through Thailand in an attempt to "find purpose." He'd studied with monks, he'd said, made friends with island dogs, and in the pictures he often showed me, curly-tailed blond mutts fetched sticks on sandy beaches while his toes poked up from the bottom frame. One fall afternoon, two weeks into dating, he lifted his shirt to show me the scar from the accident that had nearly killed him.

"Fell off a rented moped in Phuket," he said, "and it was green from infection by the time I found a doctor."

It was shiny like melted wax and curled in the shape of a crescent moon.

Those first few months we dated, I liked to tease Keith that he had crossed an entire globe just to feel rooted to the earth. He was from a quaint Massachusetts town, the kind with granite-façade public libraries and American flags hanging from every screened-in porch, and the joke was always that he would've been better off trudging in the woods behind his house than taking four planes and three small ferries to an island in the middle of the Bay of Bengal.

"It would've been a whole lot cheaper," I said, "although admittedly less exotic."

"I could've foraged for wild mushrooms," he said, "and had my own private Full Moon Party."

It wasn't until many months into our relationship that Keith revealed his trip to Southeast Asia had been triggered not by an existential need to know himself, but because his parents had recently finalized their divorce and escape seemed a necessary luxury.

"It was awful," he said. "Awful. You think, *This can't be happening.* One day I just woke up and bought a ticket. I had to get away. Thailand sounded warm and wet and wild, as far from Massachusetts as seemed possible."

It was a heartbreaking story, one I held in strangely high regard for the duration of our relationship. It seemed to me proof that Keith was loyal and dedicated, a man who willingly inverted my snow boots over the radiator to dry and plated my dinners in the shape of hearts: a Dijon-encrusted pork chop embellished with the delicate curve of a few green beans. Every other Sunday, he baked me loaves of bread—their crust dotted with plump, round raisins whose careful placement suggested eyes—and he left them outside my door with a Post-it marked with careful instructions. *Reheat me in a 350° oven,* he wrote, *and I'll get nice and crispy!*

As fraught and often difficult as Keith's childhood had been, I liked to believe that it meant something, that some good would ultimately come of it. Because Keith knew exactly what an unhappy marriage looked like, I thought he'd be avid in creating its polar opposite. He'd emerged somehow from that upbringing strong, confident, and resilient, a pillar of internal strength. My own parents had been happily married for nearly thirty years and still took romantic trips to Burlington, Vermont, or Charlotte, North Carolina, and when Keith and I would drive the three hours east from Gettysburg to spend the weekend beside them—sitting on their screened-in porch or plucking green beans from my father's garden—I always awaited our long drive home, how Keith would reflect meditatively as he stroked my wrist.

"Your parents are good people," he'd say. He always sent my mother a thank-you card.

Just as I imagined that Keith would make the ideal husband, I imagined, too, he knew I would be his wife. I liked to imagine our futures together: Keith mixing banana pancakes for our children as I wiped the mud from their light-up sneakers. When in the spring of our senior year we'd been together for three and a half years, it seemed nothing if not obvious that we should make a plan to stay together. We were still too young to get engaged, we agreed, but we could consider moving in together, getting a dog, beginning a life.

"We can buy bluebird-themed dishware," I said, "and matching Williams-Sonoma aprons."

"We can find an apartment in a sprawling city," he said. "Somewhere north, somewhere busy."

It was in the crux of all this planning—imagining throw pillows and bedspread patterns—that Keith returned to Boston to see his family, and because he wasn't there that night, it was Kevin who walked me home. And because no one saw those events coming, it was difficult, in the weeks that followed, to think of love as anything other than volatile or temperamental.

"How could he do that?" I'd often ask Keith, but he'd sigh or shake his head.

"I don't know," he'd say. "I don't know."

I was suffering and believed it was Keith's job to follow me into that darkness. But he didn't, wouldn't, did not see the point in being gone. At night, I asked him questions neither one of us felt comfortable answering—"Do you think she suffered badly? Do you think she suffered long?"—but it was only ever my attempt to spark and generate a conversation, to will a dialogue as a way to cope. And in the face of his resistance, I grew more adamant in my asking.

Later, I'd understand that Keith withdrew in those initial months not because he didn't care, but because he felt oddly familiar with the universe's unpredictability. He understood then what would take me years to figure out: that there was no way to make what had happened make any logical or emotional sense. That sometimes awful things just happened, and there was no way to predict or prevent them.

But in the same way Keith became determined to move beyond it, I became obsessed. I like to think it was because I imagined both Kevin and I had spent our childhoods in trees, in the creeks of rural Pennsylvania, lifting the front tires of our bikes over bridges the state had long ago condemned. Or perhaps because Kevin was my year, too, or because, like me, he enjoyed writing. I want to think it was born of sweetness. But whatever the reason for my fascination, I spent my nights researching potential defense strategies, the biological arguments for temporary insanity, and the handful of famous cases in which the idea of a "crime of passion" had been used successfully.

Equally compelling was the controversial nature of an abrupt withdrawal from antidepressants, long linked by correlation to violent actions, irrational thinking, and unprecedented impulsive behavior. I learned that in March of 2004, dozens of parents had testified before members of the Food and Drug Administration about their children's recent violent and erratic behavior after cessation of antidepressants. But the hearing had proved inconclusive. The FDA would only confirm that the medication—and an adolescent's sudden withdrawal—could cause "anxiety, agitation, panic attacks, insomnia, irritability, hostility, mania, aggressiveness, impulsivity." These behaviors—most specifically agitation, hostility, impulsivity, and mania—were believed to be induced as a result of the impact on the brain neurotransmitter serotonin. In fact, these reactions are identical to those instigated by PCP, methamphetamine, and cocaine—the drugs that have long been understood to cause aggression, hostility, and violence.

In 2006, an advisory committee to the FDA had recommended that medications offer an extended warning to include patients under twenty-five. Partially funded by the National Institute of Mental Health, the study was published in April of 2007, and strongly advised that children and adolescents taking SSRI medications be closely monitored throughout the duration of their treatment and immediately following the drugs' withdrawal. Patients might experience worsening of their depression, they warned, or the emergence of suicidal thinking or behavior. Furthermore, these patients were more susceptible to unusual *changes* in behavior, including but not limited to sleeplessness, agitation, and withdrawal from normal, day-to-day social situations.

An increase in anxiety seemed understandable. So, too, did insomnia, and even impulsivity, as it seemed natural that a body would adjust to changes in brain chemistry. But the idea of mania stuck out; it sticks out to me even now. Mania, I learned, often caused patients to become violent, especially when disillusioned; furthermore, manic patients could "crash" into depression and suicidal states, all the while remaining capable of carrying out elaborate and grandiose plans. In one clinical trial, six percent of children prescribed a normal dose of the antidepressant Prozac developed manic reactions; in contrast, the rate of children on a placebo sugar pill was zero.

It is difficult, of course, to calculate the likelihood of a patient who commits suicide or violent acts as a result of experienced mania, but additional stimulant effects—including irritability and agitation—affect a much larger percentage of patients: up to a third, in fact, or more. Further compounding this issue are the millions of medical professionals who don't recognize these reactions as drug-induced and mistakenly increase their patients' doses, risking disastrous results.

Because severe depression, I learned, is often caused by a profound sense of hopelessness and despair, it is commonly best addressed not by a medication at all, but by a variety of psychotherapeutic, educational, spiritual, and religious intervention choices, which first address the underlying problem, then provide deliverance through communication, through hope. Talk therapy, in particular, helps patients understand and address the way they're feeling, and how best to pacify and mediate those feelings in the future.

How are you? I might have asked. Or, when he asked if I was scared, admitted, *I, too, am terrified.*

The facts proved my friend had lost it, and I feared I was losing it, as well. I felt sick, confused by a world that seemed antithetical to the one I'd always known. My whole life, I'd believed the universe depended upon everything fitting together—a quilt of the most careful squares—but there was no fitting in what Kevin had done. There was no place for his behavior.

It seemed chaos, plain and simple.

Every now and then, it crossed my mind to look up my own symptoms: my fear, my agitation, my nightmares and obsessive thoughts. How I spent whole hours imagining Kevin's face or the only recollections I had of Emily, or the moments—however few—when I could recall them alone together. The way I felt when it was night. Or when I was in close proximity to a tub. Or with a man, or with a stranger, or with someone I did not trust.

All these symptoms, both big and small, I wished were less a part of me than they were.

But then September passed, and then October, and then November, and in the dreams I began to have, the things I loved were always destroyed. It started small, dresses, mostly, or books, but each night they grew exponentially until I was dreaming of my childhood home, torched and burning while someone inside called out. The family dog struck by a moving car. Keith's hands—always his hands—disappearing in a stream of water the way ink washes from the skin, the bones peeling back, as if dried Play-Doh, fragile, feeble, failing. I watched my high school boyfriend Chris—my first love, a skateboarder with perpetually dirty fingernails I'd dated for several years—crash his dirt bike into a tree, watched his body flung into the air, watched a helicopter lift his body from the flattened earth a monstrous and industrial predator. I began to feel spooked, and I feel spooked even now, and I remain haunted by those hours and those old affections and every home—not because of their destruction, but because of my inability to save the things that most need saving. The tree I once climbed in my front yard: how its branches burn and I can't extinguish them, how their roots twist and char and lock in the same way my limbs once locked.

I want to say that I did not make a choice between Keith, the man I loved, and Kevin, the man I increasingly feared. That that choice, in fact, found me. But my actions indicate, of course, otherwise.

You are in no way the victim, I thought, self-conscious even to myself.

And yet of course I also realized how much Kevin's actions were affecting me, whether I wanted to admit that truth or not.

8

THE IOWA WHERE I ARRIVED was a flattened valley, hot and yellow. I'd been promised acres of Midwestern farmland, valleys that stretched and rippled out for miles, but all I could see were mountainous black clouds and their violent streaks of lightning, infinite and boundless as they stabbed the dry, flat earth. My car sped across the highway, the interstate disappearing somewhere beneath me, the trees snarled along the steep embankments from where the worst summer storms had struck.

Those first few weeks I was alone, unloading boxes by myself late into the evening, swigging cheap beer bought from the convenience store a block away. It was August, and through the open windows the wind blew hot and wet. Iowa City's town population doubled when school was in session, but that was still a month away. Everything was quiet, lifeless in a way I'd never known. The silence was punctuated only by the occasional thunderstorm, which rattled life from the darkness, each more powerful than the last. The Midwest was a constant buzzing siren that summer, the tornado alarm sounding once or twice a week from a pole mounted in a park a block away, and I was alone amid those storms—both literal and metaphorical—because I'd wanted it that way. In the weeks leading up to my Iowa move, I'd increasingly withdrawn from Keith, insisting he not feel pressured to move halfway across the country. What had once been a barrage of insistence became a tempered, quiet understanding.

"We can try long-distance," I'd suggested, "so you don't have to uproot your entire life."

But alone those first few months, I found myself paranoid and scared, more lost in my thoughts than ever. In Boston, Keith worked nine-hour shifts and went for runs along the Charles. He called at night to give me updates on his mileage or the weather, the coffee shops he was visiting, how they roasted their own beans or sold almond biscotti in the shape of crescent moons.

"They're topped with lemon zest," he said, and from my place a thousand miles away, I listened to his report, waiting for my chance to speak.

"You wouldn't believe what I'm reading," I'd say, but what I meant was always *thinking*—how I was imagining an intruder holding a knife, the metallic blade catching the glint and eerie green of the glowing Midwestern moonlight.

But every time I spoke, Keith only grew silent or cleared his throat. "Why do we always have to talk about Kevin?"

he'd ask. "What's the sense in this rehashing?" He reminded me that people were always changing, adapting, that it was only natural to grow apart. "You should allow yourself," he said, "the luxury."

Later, after we'd hang up, I'd undress and stand in the shower until the hot water ran cold. I liked to feel it rush over me, imagine what was wrong as something that could be scrubbed away like dirt. My fear, panic, all that confusion—I imagined it diluting and draining downward, spiraling, traveling through a complex network of pipes and into rivers. I saw it float down the Mississippi, saw it in the surf on a beach in Mexico. I lathered my body slowly, always conscious of my feet: my toenails, red and shining, against the clean, white, empty tub.

The sirens were the nation's heartbeat, I decided: the rhythmic thumping ensuring vitality. They were a reminder that I was alive, that I was a person *who got to live.* The noise began first as a comfort, but eventually, like all things, my opinion of it began to change. I decided instead that the sirens—wailing and urgent—were a soundtrack to my fear, a physical manifestation of the nightmares I experienced as frequently in day as in night.

What happened does not affect you, I'd remind myself. *It was not you and you are* fine.

But it became difficult to remember. My mornings dragged on in eternal sleep, and when I rose in the afternoon, I found I had interest only in going for walks—winding routes that led me past white and yellow ranch homes and crumbling old Victorians. I'd stand on their well-swept sidewalks and always try to picture Keith laughing from a nearby patio, or flipping burgers, or drinking beer. What I wanted more than anything was to imagine the man I loved kicking a soccer ball across a yard, tossing a summer salad with vinaigrette—never anything more than the simple things, a glimpse into the life I'd always wanted.

Try, I told myself—a command, not a request. But the images never came in the way I'd always known them to, and eventually, I'd just give up, wander home, go back to bed.

When school began in September, teenagers moved loudly down the sidewalks, their bodies heavy and hard with liquor, and they kicked cans and smashed glass bottles. I always waited for the weight of them against my window or aluminum siding—men drunk or high or angry, men who could so easily take any number of the things I had.

There was nothing, I believed, separating my life from its violent end.

"I need you closer," I told Keith one night, my voice strained like a whisper. "I need you here with me."

But of course he couldn't just up and move. Work was work, he told me gently, and he was certain whatever I was going through would pass in the coming weeks. "It'd be reckless and unprofessional," he reminded me, "to leave my job just because you're lonely."

I understood and yet I didn't. I thought relationships meant that when finally I *did* decide to travel the world, I'd have more than island dogs to keep me company. But now I was alone, more afraid than I'd ever been, so when the break-up finally happened, it happened suddenly and without recourse—not because of the thousand miles in between us, but because of the space I'd created within my mind.

"It's the distance," I told him, knowing even as I said it that that wasn't it at all.

What bothered me, instead, was how Keith had remained unaffected—how he was calm, despite it all. In Boston, he baked loaves of bread and bought carafes of wine, carbonated his own water and took day trips to Cape Cod, and I hated him for that. I could not stand to hear his voice, so calm and devoid of fear.

It's for the best, I thought, and I didn't think much more about it.

I began to ignore his calls, ignore his emails, began investing all my money on devices I hoped would keep me safe. I bought a can of pepper spray shaped like a tube of lipstick and put my living room lights on timers. I installed alarms on every window—tiny pieces of plastic that wailed when slid apart—and took to visiting the local shooting range, watching men three times my size shoot rotting apples off terse, dry wood. Every few weeks, I'd stand in the upper level of the sporting goods supply shop, rapt behind a case of glinting weapons that cost more than my monthly rent. There was a tiny handheld revolver, a purple pistol with a hot-pink trigger.

"Can I help you?" an employee would ask, and I'd always shake my head, mouth *No*.

In truth, I fantasized about holding that gun, my fingers gripping its stony trigger. I longed to store it in my bedroom drawer, beside a flashlight and a pack of batteries, some cherry-scented ChapStick. How quickly I could grab it, fire it into the belly of an intruder, or a man creeping past my window, or a man slinking down the street.

How alive it'd make me feel. How *in control* again.

Eventually, fear gave way to anger and I began to abandon the idea of prevention altogether. It started with a man who scared me. I didn't trust him, but it was more than simply trust, because some nights, when sitting on this new man's lap, I'd look up into his eyes and see something I perceived as crazy, something wild and somehow unknowable—a glint, an insight into his mind, which I perceived as dark and mysterious—and I'd say this as if a taunt.

"There's something going on in there," I'd say, "that I can't know."

"It's true," he'd tell me, smirking, then pull me deeper into his lap, remove my top, my belt, my jeans. He'd climb on top and move above me, and I liked to feel his weight—how much more of it there was than mine. How easily he could overtake me, and what a perverse thrill to think he might.

Later, after he'd leave, I wouldn't lock my door because—well, just because.

Because I wanted to feel that danger?

Because I wanted to dare the world?

Because what Kevin had done—though I would never admit it—had somehow become my story, *my trauma*, tangled my life up in ways I still find complex and uncomfortable.

But I was there, I'd tell myself, a vain attempt at consolation. *He walked me home and then he killed her. This happened to me, too.*

Even now I can't say what I wanted, but I suspect the ugliest of truths: that in some way I wanted to allow myself the possibility of physical danger so that I might finally stake a claim in the fear I felt. Because at least then it might make sense—move my suffering beyond the periphery to the center, something tangible and real. Maybe this is why I wrote to Kevin. Already it seemed I was sacrificing, suffering, and so what else could I do but finally chase our friendship for the truth? What did it matter how ugly it felt? How much it truly scared me? How repulsed I was of *me*? I already felt a part of a mystery; I was an episode unto myself.

Tell me what happened, I wanted to write. *Don't you dare leave anything out.*

Instead I wrote detailed paragraphs about my new job, my new apartment, my life as it unfolded miles west in Iowa. *There's this black squirrel outside my house,* I wrote. *I've never seen anything like it.*

I didn't tell him about my dreams or how I fantasized about taking hold—of feeling pain or else inflicting it, of feeling the power rush back in. I wanted to flood my body until my organs burst, until they split and tore apart. I wanted to feel, in short, violence. Instead he recommended to me *East of Eden*, and I wrote back to suggest *The Road*.

Miss you, he'd always write, and *Miss you,* I'd respond.

It was only later—after class, or in my car, or in line at the grocery store—that I'd find myself running my fingers above my collarbone, my chest, my lungs, my heart, the very places where Emily suffered.

Am I capable of such rapid breaking? I'd wonder, never certain I wanted to know.

9

IT WAS A WOMAN in an office above a parking garage who eventually made the diagnosis. She wore a navy blue sweater with the faces of five yawning kittens across its front, and the buttons were small gray rhinestones that sparkled when they caught the light. I thought instantly of oysters: how only one in hundreds will ever hold a pearl.

It was pearls I had to think of, because I did not want to think about what she'd said.

This is classic repressed trauma. This is post-traumatic stress.

It was not what I wanted to hear; in fact, I would have preferred she say nearly anything else: that I was being self-indulgent, for example, which is what I'd been telling myself for months. Most days, it was the first thing that came to me as I rolled over in the midday light.

You are being self-indulgent, I'd think. *Get up and make some coffee.*

And yet there was no denying that my symptoms—as physical as they were emotional—were building gradually, worsening, that what was once two days without eating became three and then, somehow, four. Some mornings, I didn't even bother to take a shower, not for the sake of time, but because I worried that by its completion I'd be too tired to put on clothing. I'd just sit there in a cold, damp towel, watching *Judge Judy* until I fell back to sleep. Even now, I find it startling how many days I spent draped in a vintage afghan—the last thing my grandmother had made before she died—and how it seemed like the only good thing in my life, because it kept me warm through my quiet daze, kept me company for the many hours I noted nothing but the light as it changed its shape and intensity along my walls.

It was more than simple lethargy. There was an anger deep inside of me—a sharp, hard bead of light that broke each time I heard the mailman, or when the lobby door swung closed. I'd sit upright and crane my neck, certain that finally *here* was my inevitable answer, finally *here* was resolution. *Here* was the explanation I was certain would appear if only I could remain patient.

Here, I'd think, *is closure.*

Even then, a year into our monthly letters, I might have accepted that Kevin had killed Emily in a fit of rage; she was cheating on him, perhaps, and he was angry, consumed with pain. In no way would it be acceptable, excusable, or fair, but at *least* it would make some sense. That was always what it came down to: *At least* that *I could understand.* How else to accept that there may not be logic behind his crime at all, but instead a gradual breaking down? Complete and total mental upheaval?

Temporary insanity.

Somehow, over time, Kevin killing Emily had become the most important thing about me—the story line that, if pressed, I'd admit had shaped me more than anything: more than the smiley-face cheese and crackers my mother had served me after school, more than fishing beside my father on the sandy banks of the Susquehanna. The murder meant more than the family dog, more than the acres of rolling hillside, more than twenty-one years of sheltered existence before an abrupt and violent end. That night had nothing to do with me, and yet it had become my defining feature, a moment seemingly connected to my everything. It was my invitation, however indirect, to the underbelly of existence: the ugly things I'd never seen because I'd never sought them out, and for so long they'd ignored me, too.

Now they'd taken me in, and it scared me—it *still* scares me—how badly I wanted to know them. I wanted to spit, smoke, curse, drink in bars in perfect daylight. I wanted to lose the only things I had; I did not want them anymore. I wanted what was unpleasant: to invite impending danger, because no matter how hard I tried, no matter how fiercely I told myself *It wasn't you,* I couldn't think my fear away. Even now, it would be very easy to wax poetic about the despair I felt during those many months, but there is no real beauty in that pain. The truth, instead, is to admit those moments as inexhaustible, those mornings the worst I'd ever had, that pain paralyzing me into lack of movement because anything else felt, frankly, unbearable.

I'd later read in a letter composed by Emily's uncle—a letter drafted in preparation for Kevin's sentencing—that he, too, felt this sharp and incessant pain in the wake of his niece's absence.

These days, he wrote, *I'm still often caught up by a terrible longing, hearing that note ringing from an empty space where Emily is and was. You can get lost trying to drown out that note, and be numbed in its still grasp.*

And even now—even all these years later—it remains the most beautifully true thing I've ever read about the way we're affected by trauma.

A ringing that does not cease.

That morning in the woman's office, however, I didn't yet want to talk about the psychic ringing, the overwhelming fear, that incessant noise. The pain I felt still seemed foreign, not my own; it felt like someone else's altogether. I had no right, I thought, to admit or own it, and so I felt incapable of any healing. I was filled with grief, with sadness, and yet because even those emotions seemed downright selfish, it created within me certain self-loathing, which in turn punctuated my sadness, and that cycle, it seemed, had no end.

Instead, I told the woman about my cooking, my apartment, how I'd once visited the South of France. With every question she asked—every attempt at emotional honesty—I only steered the conversation further away: to my tofu sautéed with snap peas, my homemade chicken potpie, my supposed and inexhaustible normalcy. I named the dishes, all the while aware I hadn't made those things in months.

"They're delicious," I said, effusive.

There were things I would not admit, sitting in her tiny office. Like how I still owned a travel-size bottle of Keith's cologne, not because I needed to remember him, exactly, but the concept of men as kind. How—some many years prior— we'd gone on vacation together, and he'd asked me to pack it with my toiletries, a black zip-up where it wouldn't spill, and I'd kept it with me all that time, packed it in a box when I moved across the country, stowed it beneath my bathroom counter, between my sunscreen and a small lint roller. I'd kept it for one simple reason: I had no idea how long it might take until I trusted a man again. And how—at night, when I was most lonely—I'd dab it on my nightgown, or on my pillow, or my bedspread. My attempt, however small, at forcing that once-familiar comfort.

But sitting in her office, just a year after Kevin's crime, I could never say as much.

"We need to talk about what happened," she said, "about what's best now, I think, for you."

What she meant, I thought, was *Stop writing to him*. It seemed obvious even to me. I was inviting a monthly trauma every time I licked and sealed an envelope. I was quiet as she straightened, her sweater stretching easily across her frame. Her skin hugged her bones in a way I'd later associate with maternal wisdom, but that day I found her predictable, out-of-touch, and naive.

It's not that simple, I wanted to say. *Stop thinking this is simple.*

But it wasn't simple to her at all; it was I, in fact, who failed us both. I didn't want to believe in her diagnosis of PTSD for the same reason I didn't want to believe that I was suffering: because it seemed crazy. PTSD was a condition I believed could only ever afflict soldiers, those who'd been in combat, those who'd witnessed war. These were men and women who'd fought on battlefields, in ditches or deep ravines, in dust and sand and soil so red it looked burnt along its edges. They had thrown their bodies in front of trucks, or in front of bombs, or in front of bullets. They'd seen colleagues get blown apart, children with bandaged eyes, whole villages destroyed by gunfire at the hands of their closest peers. They saw armor and enemy fire and roaming missiles and artillery and I still felt, more often than not, a child. I still ate Trix most days for breakfast. I could not be suffering from their disorder.

I watched smoke rise from a church's chimney across the street, imagining its interior and empty silence, those rows and rows of empty pews. The way that space demanded nothing and how much more I'd prefer it to where I was.

"This is PTSD," she told me simply, "and it's not going to get better on its own. You need to talk about what happened. You need to start expressing the way you feel."

"Sure," I said, "okay," and when our hour ended, I left her office. On the long walk home, I navigated the city's alleyways, through winding passageways that looped behind storefronts and small-town diners and well-lit lots. Men leaned against graying dumpsters, throwing cigarette butts to the curb, and I feared them despite the daylight, despite how they only smiled in my direction.

And then I thought about my father—saw him standing on a sandy shore in a tidal pool in Maryland. It was the summer of 1995, thirteen years before that tragic evening. In my memory, I am happy: We stand together in the lilting light and the sandy breeze of the Chesapeake, collecting discarded shells trapped by the waning, warming tide. He'll later puncture a hole in them, I know—lay them out on his worktable in our basement—and then we'll turn them into jewelry, simple necklaces I can give to friends. I lean down into the water, sifting the shells clean with my bony hands. My father holds up a shell—oyster—round and rigid and opaque.

"Look," he says, gesturing, rinsing the shell again in the warm, clear water. I am eight, and so I rise up on my toes in an effort to gain a better view. My father is a scientist, and I admire him for this, and for many more reasons I don't yet know to know. "It's the sand that makes the pearl," he says. "No one ever thinks of that, but it's true."

He hands the shell to me and I hold it up against the light. It is smooth, and shines, and shimmers, producing a noisy *clunk* as I release it above my bucket.

"It's the greatest thing about them," he says—why do I remember this?—"how what we value most about a pearl is what an irritant has first rubbed smooth."

For the many months that followed, I tried to tell myself that I was becoming pearl-like; that somehow all my fear and worry would eventually shape me into something new. My reality was my sand, I decided. It was helping to rub me smooth.

Writing to Kevin had become a point of pride—a symbol of my commitment—and yet I wasn't sleeping, wasn't eating, could not find the motivation to make use of the fact that I was alive. Graduate school made it easy; twice a week, I taught an hour-long class before attending my own. I planned whole lessons around steady group work and found games online to fill the time of class. I buffered movies, loaded documentaries, played interviews so that my students would learn despite their instructor, who could not teach them.

Each night, I walked myself home through the city's pedestrian mall, past couples, young and laughing, leaning into each other, holding hands.

It could happen to you, I thought. *It could happen to any of us.*

At night, I lay in bed and thought only of Pennsylvania.

Kevin is in jail, I thought. *He is in jail, he is in jail, he is in jail.*

I'd later read that thoughts like mine are not uncommon; in fact, studies show that those involved in no-fault, fatal accidents are far more likely to receive treatment for PTSD than those who are responsible. We want an answer from the universe—someone to shake a finger at—and what we cannot take, more than anything, is to accept a lack of blame.

To admit that no one person or thing or step could've prevented what we find most awful.

Recently, in a highly publicized Canadian case, top criminal and forensic psychiatrist Dr. John Bradford—whose work entailed screening gruesome case videos of some of Canada's most sadistic criminals—admitted to suffering from severe PTSD induced by the recurring graphic footage he was forced to watch on a daily basis. He'd held a long and distinguished career as a doctor and a teacher, I read, his experience and know-how spanning decades, and had become terrifically skilled at emotionally distancing himself from the worst material. His work involved the criminal rather than the crime; his task was not to condemn or evaluate the severity of the killer's punishment but to enter that person's unique mind-set, their cognitive abilities just before they killed.

He had seen it all, Dr. Bradford told reporters, and yet, in the process of viewing footage of Canadian Air Force colonel Russell Williams sexually assaulting two young women—women Williams later killed—he began experiencing symptoms of PTSD so severe he was forced to take a leave of absence from his work. Decades of training, unparalleled experience, and even the most comprehensive understanding of the complexities and intricacies of the human mind offered him no immunity.

"To avoid publicity," he reported, "I did all [my] work at night . . . I would work with [Russell Williams] at night when there was no Joe Public around. So I'd be there until midnight, and I had thirty days to do the work. Then I had to go . . . see the tapes," he explained, clarifying that because of his intimate talks with Williams, he often knew the woman's fate far before he watched it unfold on screen. "And the tapes," he said, "are awful. They really are."

Dr. Bradford was crying, screaming, filled with agitation that caused him to lash out at his family. "I had never had an experience like that and it felt awful," he reported. "I was completely self-derogatory and beating myself up . . . I had this video show going on and on [in my mind] and I couldn't sleep. I would stay up until two a.m. to avoid going to sleep and so it was worse the next day."

In November of 2013, police officer Thomas Bean—one of the first to arrive at the scene of the December 2012 Sandy Hook Elementary School shooting in Newtown, Connecticut—also revealed that he was "permanently disabled," following a diagnosis of severe PTSD brought on by the startlingly graphic images he witnessed that December morning. A twelve-year veteran, Bean faces losing his job and pension because Newtown can only afford to pay an officer for a maximum of two years on disability before forcing their termination. Of the memories of bloodshed that plague him most, Bean responded, "Nothing could prepare you for that. The worst possible scenes you could think of . . . because all there was, was horror."

He contemplated dragging a razor across his wrist, he admitted. He can't sleep and experiences flashbacks on a daily basis. Recently, in a Connecticut store, Thomas convinced himself that his fellow shoppers were preparing a similar onslaught, and he fled in a frenzied panic.

And this, he says, is just the start.

"[That day] killed me inside," he said. "If I had my arm chopped off, [townspeople] would say, 'Oh yeah, he's hurt.' But instead they're like, 'We can sweep [this] under the rug and not necessarily have to pay, because it's not physically seen.' That's the problem with PTSD . . . people don't see it," he said.

In October of 2013, the military also admitted similar

symptoms in those responsible for firing military drones—
men and women traumatized by the images of death and
destruction that they, themselves, generated. For while the
controls are specifically designed to simulate the experience of
a video game, those at the helm remain nonetheless aware of
the reality of the events their consoles depict. Just as the finger
that touches the screen is both tangible and real, so too are the
bombs, with one operator recently estimating 1,626 deaths by
his hand alone.

And while I may not have seen the horror unfolding—did
not see Emily's body, full of life, go limp—I can imagine it in
graphic detail and find that, many days, I do. It's repulsive, certainly, fueling my lesser notions of myself, but like Dr. Bradford's mind, severely traumatized by his daily viewings, I remain
unable to disconnect the feed that loops incessantly inside my
brain. It's a horror show on mute, the images obscene and
graphic, the predominant and overwhelming sense that my
proximity is somehow relevant. This was and will forever be my
connection to that night: just one step removed, on the periphery, a few blocks away, while a woman my parallel lost her life.

It could have been me, I think, though in truth, it could've
been anyone.

The eventual need for prolonged help came in the parking lot of
a Super Walmart. It was March of the following year, bitterly
cold, and I stood juggling bags of misshapen groceries. With
one tightly gloved hand, I reached for the handle of my Toyota
Camry and it broke clean off in my tight, clenched palm. I bent

over to examine it, fumbling idly with my keys; it was smaller than I'd imagined, smooth and rounded against my cotton glove.

"I've never seen this happen to anyone," a mechanic later told me in his garage. "I mean, least of all, *a girl.*"

I'd simply gripped it too hard, he said, and it cost two hundred dollars to repair. But more important than any payment, he laughed, running a rag over his oil-stained hands, was, *Are you getting help?* "Are you talking to someone?" he asked, by which he meant *This isn't natural.* "A car handle doesn't just break apart. This is an Incredible Hulk–like problem."

"I was just preoccupied, I guess," I said. It was the most essential truth.

Still, the following week, I made an appointment, this time with another doctor whose name I thought sounded young, like me. Maybe if we were similar—at least on the outside— I'd find it easier to tell the truth. And when I showed up, and she *was* young, and the truth poured out in a strange new way, it came as no surprise when she diagnosed me with the exact same thing.

"This is PTSD, absolutely," she said—not a damnation but sudden salvation. Here, she explained, was the reason for my nightmares, my recurring panic attacks, why I felt on edge and always jumpy, why my heart sped up *now* and *now.* PTSD was why my palms were sweaty, why I bounced my foot beneath my desk, why I drummed my fingers on every table and was afraid to be alone. Here was why I could not date or listen to Michael Jackson's "Smooth Criminal"—*He came into her apartment / He left the bloodstains on the carpet*—and why I never went to the gym at night and why I drank too much wine and whiskey. I don't want to admit the reunions I skipped, the birthdays I missed, the wedding I never attended for no other reason than it was held in Gettysburg. The many debts I'm still repaying. The many friendships I've now lost.

But here, above all else, she explained, was why I still avoided a darkened bathroom: because no matter how hard I tried, I always pictured Emily's outstretched body, and no amount of blinking had ever willed that scene away.

She said her diagnosis gave me something tangible: something identifiable and known. It was a common thread I shared with others, those whose lives had also been overrun by trauma, and it didn't matter how we got there, she explained, no matter how big or small the trigger. War or no war, there was fear and stress now inside of us, and all we could do—if we were lucky, if we remained committed to showing up in every sense of those words—was learn to minimize that stress, as if exorcising a demon, a curse, as if expelling a ghost who'd somehow made a home of our human bodies.

My sensitivity, the woman explained, was likely a part of my genetic makeup, as much a part of me as the genes that dictated the color of my hair, of my eyes or my complexion, my modest height, my diminutive frame. It was not something to feel bad about, guilty about, to experience any embarrassment over whatsoever; it involved chemicals and neural pathways, she said, the open spaces between synapses and the way those microscopic tissues communicated. The only way to feel better, she explained—*truly* better—was to forgive myself for my reaction. It was *okay*, she said, to feel bad. It was *okay* to feel sad and scared. The self-loathing I'd created—its manifestations in my simultaneous urges to isolate and then excessively socialize—wasn't helping so much as harming. There was no place here, she said, for shame.

"When someone throws a baseball at your head," she said, "how do you respond?"

"I flinch," I said—the god's honest truth.

"Right," she said. "Exactly."

Like flinching, I viewed and evaluated my environment in its relation to my person—he walked me home, and then he killed her—and this response was biological, she explained, unavoidable and organic. It wasn't self-involvement that kept me troubled; it wasn't narcissism or vanity. It was an instinct to understand what had happened so as to prevent it from happening to myself.

"Some people," she said, "they don't flinch. They reach up. They catch the ball."

And like baseball—however simple an analogy—the way one experiences and processes the world is different for everyone.

It was a reprieve, a relief, a sense of absolute deliverance. For so long, I'd thought the solution was internal, and for years I'd tried to force it, fearing professional help would be too clinical, too touchy-feely, too *effusive*—an indulgence of what seemed to me an already self-indulgent problem. I wanted to feel better, but not through writing in a journal or flying east to be with family. Not through gardening or trying acupuncture or volunteering at an animal shelter. I knew this because I'd tried it all. I'd also tried getting drunk, getting high, going for drives late into the night, and sleeping with a man I did not trust. I'd ridden a train to San Francisco and made an appointment with a voodoo priest and visited the apartment of a man named Dodo, whose every possession was the same shade of brown, and I did not leave even when he offered me "potpourri"—his unique blend of heroin—though I was smart enough to decline his offer. I'd spent my time in dimly lit, dingy bars with people whose stories were worse than mine, because nothing that I've yet found compounds depression quite so acutely as seeing your own particular blend of unhappiness registered on the face of a perfect stranger.

It was a comfort—how similar.

I'd read, too, every study I could find on memory, mental illness, dissociation, had browsed for guns and held a rifle and dreamed of getting a tattoo of my hometown—the thin, intricate lines signifying the only place where I still felt safe—and yet that sadness still remained. That fear would not be shaken. And what it meant, the woman asserted—what I should see as indicative—was that what was going on inside of me could not care *less* about what I did.

"You need to see me once a week," she said, "or more, if you think you'll find it useful. The most important thing, though, is you need to start talking about what happened."

In the interim, she prescribed an antidepressant she hoped would provide relief. Like all antidepressants, she explained, citalopram interacted differently in everyone. I might feel worse before I felt better.

I did. Late into that third evening, not knowing what else

to do, I arrived at the doorstep of a friend, asking if I might sit on his empty couch because I did not trust myself to be alone.

"I'm weary," I told him simply.

What I meant was, *I'm not myself*, and the next morning, in an emergency appointment, I confided this to my doctor, saying, "That was the worst I've ever felt, *ever*."

And then of course I had to ask.

"What would it be like . . ." I paused. "Let's say someone had built this medicine up in his body, and he just stopped taking it, cold turkey?"

"It could get bad," she told me, "bad. It could get very, very bad."

For as much as she occupied my subconscious, I didn't think directly of Emily much until a man tried to break into my apartment. It happened on a night it rained in a way it hadn't in some time, but the sound I awoke to at three was not thunder, but an urgent, desperate pounding. Outside, the sky was bruised and black, the lightning flashing long enough to illuminate thick clouds in the inky darkness, and it pulled me from a dream like a boat tugged slow from water.

"Let me in," someone yelled from the front of my apartment building. "You better fucking *let me in*."

From my own apartment door's gauzy peephole, I could make out the figure of a man just beyond the building's entrance—his shoulders slumped in the pouring rain, his arms raised as if to attack. He was bigger and clearly older than me. He did not belong inside my building.

Immediately, my mind turned to Kevin—the things I knew a man could do if he climbed in a window or shattered glass. If he somehow made it in, mine would be the first apartment he would try; it was closest to the building's entrance, which was just feet from the door he now stood against. I checked the lock to make sure I'd secured it, then pulled a knife from a bamboo block.

"Let me in!" he called again, and from my place inside the kitchen, I could hear a sound like shattering—the glass giving way to the man's fist and weight. I imagined his fingertips, bloody, the places they might go if he made it in.

In the bathroom—the only interior room that offered a lock—I took a seat on the side of the tub and studied the door's mechanism. Its lock was old and rusty, the product of a long-ago restoration. I had no idea if it even worked. I flipped open my cell phone, pressed the numbers I'd never had to press.

When the 911 operator picked up, he was calm. He told me that the police would be notified and would arrive as soon as possible.

"I mean it," I said, my voice urgent. "He broke the glass, even."

I thought the operator would keep me on the line, would tell me exactly what I should do. I'd seen it on TV a thousand times before. Instead, he said the police were on their way, and with a click, the line went dead.

Out front, the man began to scream. He was wild. From the bathroom, I could see him as he made his way to my front window, surveying the glass before he pushed against it. It did not give, but clearly could.

"Let me in," he yelled again, and again I raised my phone.

"I'm serious," I said. "I'm calling you back because I don't think you understand. He's trying to *break* this window. He's going to come inside and he's going to kill me."

You don't know what I've been through, I wanted to say. *You don't know how afraid I am.*

Instead I said, "Please." I said, "The police *need* to get here quick."

"I have word they're on the scene," he said, but they weren't—out every dark window was more darkness; there were no lights, no sirens, no holsters, no red or blue or man.

And then, suddenly, there was. I saw first one police car pull up and then another, saw the man run across my yard, saw the policemen tackle him to the ground and secure his wrists in handcuffs. They interviewed him for forty minutes before finally lowering him into the backseat, and I watched them from my darkened kitchen, too afraid to open the refrigerator for fear the room would go aglow with light. The man might see me, and then return.

When finally they left, I returned to bed but couldn't sleep. I rose and made pancakes, eating them on my couch, watching the cartoons the cable company airs when they know no one is watching.

Somehow, in the months before, everything had seemed simple: Kevin was a friend, and he was in jail because of what he'd done. I'd never really thought of Emily. But now, hours later, I remained too afraid to pull the blinds because it meant standing beside the window. I watched the sun rise over the horizon, students move slowly across the sidewalk, their bodies alive and lit with light.

Was this the fear she felt, I thought, *waiting for help that never came?*

And I could think of Emily and wonder, because for me, help had arrived.

That man had been arrested, and I sat alive and in pajamas.

I suppose that's when it happened, the exact moment the flip got switched. Even now, I cringe at the transformation that occurred in me seemingly overnight. How it took knowing the vulnerability of my own life to understand the brutality of how hers ended. I'd later learn from a policeman taking measurements outside my building's front door that my intruder had been a kid—eighteen, nineteen years old at most.

"He seemed so big," I said.

"He was," he said. "Sure, I could see that."

His name was Henry and he was drunk, the policeman explained. He thought my house was his own. He'd been charged with public endangerment and would later appear in the city court, but in the meantime had been released on the stipulation that he pay a hefty fine for the damage incurred on my front door.

"I'm just taking measurements," the officer said simply.

The fact that the intruder—a man I'd imagined as thirty or forty at least—was markedly younger didn't change very much; the fear I'd felt was no less urgent, real, or threatening. And again it drew that parallel: a young man overcome, responding with violence.

"He'll pay for the damage," the officer said, "but we have no reason to think he would have hurt you."

He said this as a comfort and because, of course, he couldn't know I'd lost my trust in reason months ago.

10

I AM AWARE—AND ALWAYS HAVE BEEN—that Emily's trauma is not my trauma. Her murder is not my own. And yet I've found in these past few years, I've become increasingly desperate to learn and know her.

These urges come to me naturally and in the most inconvenient of places: while waiting in line at the car wash, while listening to a country song about a splintered porch. And if I was a braver person, I think, I might've attempted to meet her family. I might've attempted to speak with her only brother. I would have driven to their New Jersey home and asked to sit beside them on their couch, a ceiling fan spinning dizzily above us, and then perhaps I might come to learn her, as if to undo my former indifference.

"What's her favorite food?" I'd ask, and then I'd ask if we could make it.

But I am terrified to contact her family; I am terrified to show up at their home. My association—and continued association—with Kevin feels nothing if not awful, especially when I think of them. I think of them and I think, *Shit.* I think, *What are you doing, writing the man who killed her?*

But the problem remains simple: The Kevin who killed Emily is the same man who walked me home first.

And yet everything I feel for Kevin, I feel for Emily and her family threefold. But it is troubling, of course, to admit that she was a girl I never knew, a girl I never even tried to know because she was three years younger and that, somehow, mattered. I was a senior who spent her evenings in bars and restaurants and in the pub near the downtown rotary, ordering beers and sweet red wine. And because in Pennsylvania Emily couldn't even sit at our table if we ordered alcohol, she likely felt too awkward to ever join us. In one of the only memories I have of her, in fact, she's standing beside Kevin at my twenty-first-birthday party—held at the brewery a mile away—while a waiter leans down gently to tell her she cannot sit at our gigantic table.

"I'm sorry," he says politely, "but this lady's ordered a flight of beer."

It was never that I was purposefully indifferent to Emily, but that my attention was always elsewhere: my studies, my friends, the places I hoped to go. Even when she and Kevin started dating, I thought that I'd soon leave Gettysburg, and leave Pennsylvania, and cross the country or an ocean or go to I don't know where, but in no way did I anticipate it mattering who Emily was or might have been.

This is what I thought, whether I feel comfortable admitting that truth or not.

It was just that Emily was still so young, with so many years and experiences ahead of her, and in the worlds I've since imagined, she's working as a foreign diplomat, or she's on a plane above an ocean. She's heading to northern Africa to teach English in a clean, bright classroom.

The night he killed her, she and Kevin had been dating off and on for seven months, and I didn't think of her for the nearly three years after because it seemed to me all but impossible.

There was already one wall of grief around my heart; I could not stand to build another.

Instead, I let those years pass slowly, quietly, subtly, without ever reaching out to her friends or family. I never wrote anyone the sort of letter I had sent as a child to absolute strangers. I tried so hard not to notice her absence, in fact, that time's accumulation seems to me now devastating. Three years is the same amount of time, I learned recently, that it takes a child from birth to understand puzzles, sort objects logically, recognize emotions, form conscious friendships. How long it takes a peach pit to become a fruit-bearing tree, how long it takes an average American male to propose, how long a betta fish typically lives.

Three years. And because I didn't want to think about what Kevin had done or, more specifically, who he had done it to—not really, anyway—I spent that time instead studying thunderstorms, reading Hemingway, touring the Philippines. I taught myself to spackle and caulked a sink and tilled a garden. In a western desert, I pitched a tent. I learned Tagalog. I saw a waterspout.

In a small town in Illinois, I split dessert with the nation's best juggler.

In a small town in eastern Iowa, I kissed Flavor Flav on his stubbly cheek.

In an island in the South Pacific, I sat on a bar stool while a woman ran a bamboo shoot across my body—again and again and again—and I waited as she blew in, blew out, blew in: her native attempt to undo a curse. "Has it been there long?" I asked, bewildered, and she lowered her eyes, not knowing my language.

Three years, and every night I climbed into bed hoping I'd have no energy left to dream of Emily, but of course I always did: I saw her taking notes in some sunlit classroom, or writing stories, or reading books. Other nights, I dreamt I was hovering somewhere above her, descending that rusty fire escape and running barefoot down the sidewalk to arrive in her darkened bedroom before the letters could arrive in the soft, brown mulch. Those testimonies to her memory, to how much she truly mattered.

I stood beside her body, still alive and flush with sleep, and I tugged gently at her smooth, warm wrist. Miles away, on the battlefields, far from all that danger, we sprawled out on our backs to stare up at the bright, white moon. We imagined patterns in the stars, and I pointed my finger upward, saying, *Ursa Major, Ursa Minor.*

My dreams always began the same—with darkness and a quilt of stars—but in every dream, I stayed beside her. In every dream, I kept her safe.

"Just a little longer," I always said, and I waited beside her for night to end.

In the only other memory I have of Emily, she's drinking red wine from a Solo cup, standing in the hallway of my apartment, just six months before her murder. It's Halloween, and she's Kevin's new girlfriend—a purple fairy with nylon wings—and I ask her to take my photograph. I nudge her, hold up my camera, and say, "Please?" I say, "Would you mind?"

I pose beside a referee, a soccer player, and a banana.

Of the many photos of that night, Emily is only ever the glittering black wings in the background of my posing. Me, beside a cupcake decorated like a spider. Me, beside a pumpkin. Me, dressed in yellow, a flirty bumblebee in black high heels.

I had no way of knowing then that many years and a thousand miles removed from that night, that town, that world, I'd think of Emily often and find myself wondering the simplest things.

How she liked to eat her spaghetti.

If she ever had a dog.

I wonder now if Emily had ever been to Europe, or if she wanted to go, or what color she'd paint her toenails if she was around to paint them now. In the most difficult moments, I find myself hoping that Emily saw the Pacific Ocean before she died, or Yellowstone, or the Grand Canyon at the very least. Recently, while on a road trip across the country, I stood on the edge of that dusty basin, all the endless red rock below, and thought, *I hope that Emily saw this.*

I have no idea, of course, what Emily did or did not see, because the same distance that kept me from knowing Emily in life kept me from learning her after her death.

"It's not like you were friends," someone told me once in an attack I never refuted but will never forget. "So it's scary, sure—that proximity—but you don't have a claim in all this sadness."

As if sadness is an entity one seeks desperately to call one's own.

I grieve, then, in absolute private. Occasionally—maybe once a month—I find myself navigating to Emily's online memorial and the nonprofit organization her parents founded in her name. The Emily Fund, it's called, and their slogan is *Do one thing.*

"Choose one or a few dates during the year to raise awareness about the social issues that most move you," the website reads, and then there's a pop-up calendar with sixty dates: ideal opportunities for making a difference. *Find the cause that matters most*, I read, and then I consider them quietly:

March 1: Energy Day; day the Peace Corps was founded in 1961
July 26: Americans with Disabilities Act signed in 1990
December 1: Antarctic Peace Treaty established in 1959

Pick your cause, I think. *Do something*, except I never do.

Every time I look at them, they startle me into lack of movement: how there are all these things I could be doing while I otherwise just sit and think of her.

Elsewhere on the page, I can browse photographs of Emily—whole pages in an online archive forever logged for our memory. I can learn her retroactively, and many nights I do: I see Emily eating a marshmallow from a stick in her Brownie uniform, or clutching her skirt on a sandy boardwalk. She's sitting in a pile of leaves, her hair tucked into a bright green jacket, and the fur trim is pulled up and around her face, her lips puckered in the expression of someone who trusts they will live a long, safe life.

Her eyes are wide and lively. Her skin is full of color.

It is the world of Emily I never knew, that I never even tried to know, and it's all I'll ever get because I still remain too upset to ask for more. What right would I even have?

She was nineteen the night she died. Five blocks away, I was asleep.

What happened ultimately—it seems too simple a resolution.

For eighteen months, Kevin and Emily's family and his family and everyone waited: for a trial, for a verdict, for the many answers to the many questions that remained. *Why was Emily there that night? What could have happened to set him off? And was it even possible—temporary insanity, a crime of passion?*

Then, quietly, on an afternoon in October, Kevin wrote to say his lawyer had agreed to a plea deal that eliminated the possibility of a life sentence but mandated, instead, twenty-seven to fifty years in a maximum-security prison. He would remain ineligible for parole until he was forty-nine years old, at least, but all things considered, he said, it was a gift, a reprieve.

It's better this way, he wrote.

A public trial would have proved arduous and emotionally taxing, would have ripped raw the wounds that in eighteen months had begun to heal. He would spend the rest of his life doing as much good as he possibly could, he read from a speech the day of his sentencing, and said he found himself wishing every single day that he could've traded places with Emily.

He said, "I never meant to hurt her."

Now, with sentencing behind him, he could finally be moved to a more permanent facility—"my new home," he called it simply—where he could take up a routine schedule, enroll in classes, and assume a part-time job. And while I wanted to feel relief—a friend would be relieved—in truth, I was devastated. Without a public trial—without the testimonies of trained professionals, mental health specialists, and Kevin's own confessional statement—I'd have no way of knowing whether the night had unfolded as he claimed, if truly, in that moment, he had "no idea" just what he had done. It was what I needed to hear the most—that the violent thing he'd done was honestly beyond his control.

I thought—naively—I could seek it through email. Distance seemed, if anything, a luxury. *Why a plea deal?* I wrote his lawyer. It was an act of brazen inquiry, but one I hoped could provide the answer. Was there evidence, however small, that could prove particularly incriminating?

When two days later his lawyer replied, his response was startlingly simple.

It was a very difficult situation for all involved, he wrote. *We are somewhat happy that Kevin will have a significant part of his life left when he is released from incarceration, [but] of course, all are greatly saddened by the loss of Ms. Silverstein. The final court proceedings were very difficult, as members of both families suffered greatly.*

But in their suffering, had they gained closure? And could it be afforded to me, too?

It was what I needed most, however self-indulgent or obsessive, and if it meant seeking it out myself—returning to the origin of that nightmare, shining a light on what haunted me most—it seemed the least I could do, so I canceled my plane ticket home for Thanksgiving and rerouted my trip to Gettysburg.

The drive east took eighteen hours. I saw flattened terrain, vibrant meadows, dust devils churning in empty fields and the steely gray propellers of wind turbines strapped to eighteen-wheelers. I spent the night in Ohio, eating pork loin fried auburn.

It was strange to be back. The years had been long ones, and it felt strange—how anticlimactic my return. The town and the campus buildings couldn't have felt any less familiar—the students seemingly unaware of the murder, just two years before. They laughed and sucked on Starbucks straws, threw Frisbees across the quad. The Gettysburg I'd left was still in mourning; there were signs and flowers in nearly every yard.

There were pictures and camera crews and anchorwomen and boxy vans, and I somehow expected them to all still be there, as if preserved throughout these past two years, repeatedly thawed and again frozen to ice. I'd imagined leaves falling onto the posters, then disintegrating under snow, and how on the first warm day of spring, the ink would appear unaffected, the paper firm.

At the front desk of campus security, I inquired about parking.

"Reason for your visit?" the guard asked.

What *was* my reason? It was something not even I could say. Whether for emotional relief or a sense of validation or answers, however difficult—there no longer seemed a discernible difference. What to tell this man who expected I had come for photographs, to pose beside the buildings where I'd once lived, learned, slept, and ate? I stood before him in a dress—soft yellow linen the heat made cling—and I imagined what he perceived as my nostalgia. My naiveté and still-young innocence.

Because I was friends with the man who, years ago, brutally killed that young lady, I thought but did not say. I studied his face, the way the skin folded around his eyes like turnovers, soft and doughy and round.

"Memories, I guess," I said.

I had promised myself—for the sake of my sanity—that I'd head directly to the courthouse. I did not want to see the cafeteria or the chapel where we'd met, the brick row home we'd shared with others or the campus green where we'd lie out, smoking cigarettes and people-watching, texting others *Hey, come join us.*

I did not want—even minutely—to remember the annual concert he'd established as a way of promoting local bands just a month before his arrest. The concert was named, simply, "The Spring Concert," and it exists even now; every April, the same month our lives all changed, students gather on towels and blankets to fling Frisbees in bikini bottoms and cargo shorts, wave their hands to the hypnotic rhythm of bass guitars and overly earnest lyrics. Two years later, that concert is—and likely forever will be—a more tangible and physical presence than Kevin, its founder, himself.

I really miss discovering new music, he wrote once, *but at least now I have radio.*

The point of my visit, in other words, was not to reengage a trauma, and yet of course I had to see it again—the bench they'd bought for her. I found it in the heart of campus, just beside that grassy swell, pinwheels still churning in the air beside it, the daffodils alive, I knew, but dormant, their death only temporary.

My love, she laughs like the flowers, an engraving read, and I tried to remember the rest, the subsequent lyrics to that song. I couldn't remember its title, or its artist, only that it had something to do, I thought, with a bridge, a holding station, a train or bus.

"Valentines can't buy her?" I asked aloud, but of course there was no one there to answer.

The bench made me want to see Kevin's house and the battlefields, exactly as I knew it would. Outside, on the front porch, a woman lay in a white hammock, a jug of sun tea steeping beside her, and I parked my car along the shoulder and waited for the fear to rush over me, a sensation I was certain would come, and quickly. Or maybe the opposite; I'd see the house once so familiar and be instantly betrayed by my better instincts, feeling happiness instead. Though it wasn't fear or joy that came; it was a profound and harrowing longing. I imagined the woman in the hammock rising to her heels and greeting me, offering consolation on the sidewalk, and I'd be grateful as I wrapped my arms around her, as I explained the terrible thing that had happened.

This house, I'd say, *a murder.*

But who was to say she didn't know? And what right did I have to tell her? She'd managed to make a home where others had left only tragedy, and I admired her for that—how that front porch offered solace, offered peace.

From the house, it was an easy half mile to the battlefields. I shifted my car back into drive and let it glide across the asphalt, felt the wheel rock beneath my palms. Their proximity was once Kevin's favorite thing about where he'd lived: how he could look out at them at night. At Devil's Den, I parked the car and climbed the rocks, holding my dress up as my knees stretched out. The sun was hot, casting yellow, watery light across a place where I now felt everything: love and hate and fear and trepidation for what this town meant. In the distance, the last battlefield bus kicked up dust, and I watched it until it disappeared, scuffing pebbles until they fell, until they bounced and came to rest along the battlefields, the softened earth.

I know now that the song quoted on Emily's bench is Bob Dylan's, and that it's called "Love Minus Zero / No Limit." The implication, of course, is of a love that remains whole— nothing can be retracted because nothing ever can be. Love is love is love, and who can say where it goes when it goes?

My love, he sings, *she speaks like silence, without ideals or violence.*

My love, he sings, *she's like some raven at my window with a broken wing.*

To heal—a wing or worry—I thought meant, above all, *closure,* so in the Adams County Courthouse an hour later, I unloaded my pockets into plastic bins and asked a receptionist what was available.

"Public records, I mean," I said. "Anything you might have on Kevin Schaeffer."

She retreated into the back and I thought of Kevin; I hadn't told him of my planned visit for reasons I worried would complicate our interaction. We had a rule, however unspoken, that mandated an avoidance of discussing mental illness, of talking about what had happened, of talking about his own account. Everything else was on the table and available to me as such, but there seemed a quiet understanding that I wasn't to inquire about Emily or that April night or how he felt or continued to feel. And it was a rule I'd long felt comfortable with when the case was still ongoing, but now that things were final, it seemed an unnecessary impediment. It bothered me: how, on principle, I was free to ask him anything, and he was, ostensibly, free to answer. And yet inquiring seemed to betray the parameters of our friendship, rules I myself had set by being complicit in my quiet behavior.

Reading the comprehensive paperwork in private, without his knowing, seemed a necessary withholding, an earned sort of luxury. And anyway, Kevin was no longer in Gettysburg; he'd been moved, following his plea deal, to a facility twenty-five miles north, in Camp Hill, which served as the state's only diagnostic and classification center for men, a sort of boot camp for inmates to acclimatize them for relocation. He would be there for three, maybe four weeks, he said, before being moved to SCI Albion, the state's northernmost facility, just thirty miles from the shores of Erie. Albion would be the farthest from home Kevin would ever live, the farthest from Oley he could even be placed. It was a straight, diagonal line across the state, a full day's drive for his aging parents.

But he'll be safe there, his mother wrote me, *and that's what's most important.*

And yet when the receptionist returned from her back office, the pile she handed me was several hundred pages high. Here was an autopsy report, a list of evidence, Kevin's detailed statement of confession. Testimonies to his mental state and character. Annotated notes on his childhood.

It was material that would take weeks, if not months, to sort through, and because of the particularly sensitive nature, it wasn't a task I wanted to do within the confines of the public courthouse. The last thing I wanted to do was sit beside other people while they looked up the darker parts of their lives. But I could have it photocopied, the receptionist offered politely. It wouldn't even cost that much.

"How long will that take?" I asked.

"One week," she told me simply.

I'd expected longer. I'd expected at least a month. I thought to photocopy the entire criminal case as presented to me in the Adams County Courthouse and mail the files to Iowa would take the work of many people, the patience and photocopying skills of only the best secretary in Gettysburg. I imagined long hours and red stamps conceding the DA's approval. There was an inventory of confiscated evidence, after all, what'd been taken from his bedroom. There was a search warrant for his car and another for his hard drive, mental health evaluations, and every admission he'd ever made while in custody for the past eighteen months.

"Oh," I said. "Okay."

It cost just over a hundred dollars, and when she called, days later, to confirm the extent of all I wanted, I was surprised by her easy nature.

"You want the plea deal transcript?" she asked.

"Yes."

"His mental health evaluation, as presented to the district attorney?"

"Yes."

"The statements by her mother? By her father? Her only brother?"

"By whom?" I asked.

"Emily's," she said. "By her cousins? Her uncle? Her aunt?"

"They're there?" I asked, quiet. "There are statements from her aunt?"

"To attest to the grieving. To attest to everything they've lost."

"Oh."

"This is all very standard," she said. "They're collected to influence his sentencing."

I swallowed. "Then yes," I said, though I couldn't imagine how they'd make me feel. "I can't believe," I said finally, "that these are public record."

"Well," she said, and sighed.

"Then yes," I said. "I guess so. I mean, I need all of it. Send all of it." Then I thanked her and hung up the phone before I had the chance to change my mind.

And yet when a week later they arrived, I was surprised by their timeliness. I took a seat at the kitchen table and tried to will the envelope open.

Come on, I thought, *come on.*

Inside were documents I knew I wouldn't feel right examining, and while ordering them had seemed one thing, it seemed another altogether that they were, finally, on my counter—to know that with such ease I could give new life to a two-year-old story. It seemed grossly inappropriate but nevertheless necessary: I had to go through everything, the hundreds and hundreds of papers, some handwritten and others typed, because how else could I claim to understand the situation—gain closure or glean meaning—if I couldn't look at all that'd happened? If I couldn't read those detailed letters?

How could I ever attempt closure, or forgive Kevin, or forgive myself by proxy if I couldn't bring even myself to look at them? But days stretched into weeks and still the files remained unopened. It was the most beautiful limbo: a safe, in-between space where I could feel good about my bravery without the risk and guilt of invasion. Each night, I'd run a sponge over my dinner plates, dishwater splashing up onto the folder, and I'd run a rag over its smooth, beige surface, carefully blotting the water stains, but still it remained unopened.

It's too late for that tonight, I'd think. *I'll have nightmares if I read it now.*

In the morning, the light will be better, I'd think. *In the morning, I won't be afraid.*

Come morning, I would no longer be a single, young female in a dark house alone on a quiet street. The birds would be out. The sun would be shining, maybe.

It was *Law & Order* that finally set me off. Late into the evening, I watched as two detectives made their way through the woods, then loaded a body into an ambulance. In a dark and dimly lit basement, a coroner sliced into a woman's torso, and the camera panned over the victim's blue feet, her skin translucent and nearly purple. The body was big and bloated stiff, and the camera panned up slowly, revealing her thighs and chest and neck, and when at last the victim's head came into sight, the skin itself was peeled, her face a human orange.

"What," I said aloud, frantically reaching for the remote. In the apartment next door, a dog began to yip, spinning himself in dizzy circles, alarmed by the invisible danger, and so, too, was I, because it was not what I'd envisioned when I'd envisioned an autopsy. It was not what I thought at all. An autopsy, I thought I knew, involved only small incisions—tiny sutures, tiny wounds, injuries less than an inch in diameter. When I imagined Emily's body lowered into her final resting spot, I'd only ever imagined stitches, microscopic samples, a scalpel as thin and subtle as a fingernail, only the most minute little abrasions. It was a coroner's job, I thought, to indicate the cause of death and to clarify exactly what had happened so as to serve Emily and her family justice. But his job, too, to repair what Kevin had so badly broken. To stitch up every wound, return Emily her normality. That was what I thought: that at least in the physical sense, the autopsy undid the damage Kevin had caused.

And yet the scene on the television was anything but clean. It was thoughtlessly graphic, an image meant to entice the at-home audience. In the kitchen, I typed *autopsy* into my computer, frantic, scrolling through the search hits, each site more graphic than the last.

How stupid and naive, I realized, *to consider it somehow* clean. *To think it involved* fixing.

To realize how horrific and tragic even Emily's autopsy must have been.

The violence was not over just because Kevin turned himself in to the police. It was made worse after the worst, before finally made clean for her funeral. Her autopsy—the very thing I naively believed somehow set things right—had only damaged her further. It was not at all like stitches.

It was nothing in the world like some tiny, final wound.

. . .

I know now that Emily suffered massive hemorrhaging, fingernail-shaped abrasions, marks "consistent with manual strangulation" in addition to her wounds. There was discoloration on her eyelids, cuts on her forearms, hands, and wrists.

There was blunt force trauma to her head and neck.

There was evidence of a struggle.

At the time of her death, she was wearing blue velour sweatpants, a tie-dyed hooded sweatshirt, and a gold shirt that read FOREVER, and for many months, this was the most I knew about Emily. There's something very difficult in obtaining that sensitive knowledge: the exact way in which a person died. Their death begins to take precedence over who they were, or the person you wished you'd found the time to know, and while I'd acquired the documents for a sense of closure, I found they only opened my wound further. The regret was as swift as it was crushing, emerging even before I took my eyes off the paper.

The only thing I could do, I decided, was bury that new knowledge under more new knowledge, so I began to seek out new things—details and characteristics as irrelevant to her death as perhaps they were in life.

I learned she liked watermelon.

That her favorite sport was swimming.

That in high school she participated in the Model United Nations, and in a photo I've found online, she's waving a flag at Liberia's table.

She was vegetarian, a Cancer, a member of Amnesty International. She pitched tents in the middle of our college campus to raise awareness for homelessness, and in the sixth grade, she wrote the president. I like to imagine what she'd said.

Emily liked art—most recently, creative writing—and was slowly learning Arabic. She was apple-cheeked and a brunette and spent her summers working at Dairy Queen, twisting vanilla soft-serve into plastic cups. In nearly every photo I've found, she's wearing a different pair of neon sunglasses, and while I can't say I've ever believed in heaven—I'm not certain I do, even now—if it's there, she must be in it, surrounded by all of those who came before her. I imagine an eternal and blazing summer, a wet, orange dusk in late July, the heat rising, wafting in waves above the pavement, Emily laughing, her sunglasses on.

The same minute she was dying, two hundred and fifty others were being born, and I don't know how existence works, how one life does or does not fold into another. Two hundred and fifty others, and it gives me great comfort to think of them.

11

THERE IS NO RATIONAL EXPLANATION for what I now suspect is true: that in an attempt to justify our ongoing communication, my mind began to form new memories of Kevin—a whole archive of moments we may or may not have shared—and to this day, I have no idea whether they happened with him or with someone else.

The night that we went ghost hunting on the battlefields, for example—this was my favorite thing I think we did. But of course I'm no longer certain if it was even Kevin beside me that night; it could have been Sam, or Eric, or Anthony, or someone else altogether. And while there are a number of mutual friends who, if I called them, might confirm it—"Was that him?" I could ask. "Or was that you? And how've you been?"—I have no interest in verification. I find myself grateful for the ambiguity. It allows me to think that, yes—yes, *of course*—that occurred with Kevin.

Here was just one of many nights, I think, *of good, clean, harmless fun.*

Because I've done the research, I understand how it can happen. Studies show that a disproportionate amount of memories are stored during early adolescence—ten to thirty years old, in fact—as the memories logged within their period are most crucial to the formation of self-identity. Traumas that occur within this time frame are therefore recalled especially more vividly for precisely the same reason: they shape who we become. Over time, these memories may override what otherwise exists within that space: memories of Kevin laughing, for example, pulling Pop-Tarts from a toaster. It's called the theory of flashbulb memory, and it explains, I think—or tries to—why the fact our four-year friendship does not align with the meager number of memories I now have.

There is also the theory of cognitive dissonance, which states that the very things that we hold true can—and will—begin to shift if in direct conflict with our behavior. It's an anxiety response, much like the child sitting on my chest, the feeling of tiny feet toeing softly through my rib cage. I cared and continued caring—even long after I learned the truth—and so my mind adjusted accordingly. It fabricated moments that were sufficiently pleasant.

Now I want to believe my memories occurred with Kevin because I need to believe they did. How else to justify my monthly letters or the illustrations he often sends? In one, the *A* of my name curls upward, a fairy-tale sort of font, framed by a wall of ivy and, behind it, a neon sun. There needs to be justification, a litany of memories as to why I care, so my brain began stitching a patchwork, a colorful arrangement of memories, inserting Kevin into peaceful places where I'm not certain he belongs, and whether or not they're real seems arbitrary to me entirely.

For all intents and purposes, writes famed neurologist Oliver Sacks in his 2013 essay "Speak, Memory," they may as well be real. One of the nation's top researchers on the formation of memory, Sacks writes that "even if the underlying mechanism of a false memory is exposed, [it] may not alter the sense of actual lived experience or reality such memories have. Nor, for that matter, may the obvious contradictions or absurdity of certain memories alter the sense of conviction or belief."

Once a memory is constructed—accompanied by vivid sensory imagery and strong emotion—there is no longer an inner, psychological way of distinguishing what's true from false. Or any outer, neurological way.

Sacks writes that even when examined using functional brain imaging technology, studies show that vivid memories produce widespread activation in the brain's sensory areas, emotional (limbic) areas, and executive (frontal lobe) areas—a pattern that is "virtually identical whether the 'memory' is based on experience or not."

As sophisticated as its structure may be, no mechanism within the brain ensures the truth of our recollections. There is no way by which the events we experience can be objectively catalogued within our mind. They are experienced and constructed in a highly subjective way, Sacks explains, unique to every individual, and are reinterpreted or reexperienced differently every single time they're recollected.

The only truth then, he writes, is narrative—the stories we tell ourselves.

He walked me home, and then he killed her.

It's convincing enough for me, however clinical it might seem; there is comfort in cold facts and data. And it explains an ugly truth, one I've disregarded since learning it: how, at some point in my reading of the official records, I learned I was not the last person Kevin saw at all—he admitted to police in his initial confession that he visited our friend Wilson after me, and they watched television for thirty minutes before he finally headed home. It should, you'd think, change everything, but it did not, could not, change the narrative I'd created within my mind. For two years, I believed I was the last person to see him—the last woman before Emily—and it's not a concept I can now withdraw or retract in any manner.

It sounds ludicrous, I realize, and worse, there's no way to explain it to someone who hasn't experienced something similar: how the lies we tell ourselves begin to feel more, in time, like truth.

So, real or else imagined, it was a Monday when we snuck out—we knew the park rangers wouldn't be patrolling. They drove through the battlefields heavily on Friday nights, shining their flashlights over the flat green earth to reveal drunken fraternity brothers peeing on cannons or posing for indecent photos with the obelisks, and Saturdays could be bad as well, but on a weeknight those fields were clear.

"Feel like getting scared?" Kevin—I think Kevin—asked, and I laughed and said, "You're on." I said, "Those battlefields don't scare me."

Kevin always liked feeling close to history—"It's dark enough," he said, "to imagine war"—but for me, the battlefields were only ever an opportunity to stumble around like a child, drunk and alive and giddy, shining my flashlight over boulders as I took narrow swigs from a pocket flask. The week before this memory, in fact, Keith had bought me my very own: stainless steel with a pink leather trim, my initials carved across its frame in a cursive script I found condescendingly feminine. I filled it that night with cheap tequila, using a funnel meant for motor oil, then sliced a lime into careful wedges and placed them in a sandwich-size Ziploc. I had stolen an upright saltshaker from the cafeteria at dinner, and when at last I joined him on the sidewalk, Kevin was leaning against a streetlamp, his head tucked inside his shirt, a modern-day Headless Horseman.

"You're not going to scare me," I said, laughing, and he popped his head out, bit by bit.

"I know," he said, defeated.

Above us, the sky spread open like a welt, the last bits of daylight folding softly into the horizon. I clicked my flashlight on to illuminate shadows in the inky darkness. The moon shined golden over the roadway, and with every oncoming car, we pulled our hoods up and stepped to the shoulder.

"Easy," Kevin said, reaching his arm out in an offer of protection. "Easy, Amy, easy."

With those hoods up, we could've been anyone, and there was a certain thrill in this. So maybe it doesn't matter—Kevin, or Sam, or someone else.

"I feel like a ghost myself," I said. "Like I'm looking for something to haunt."

"Funny," Kevin said, smirking. He raised his flashlight to his narrow chin. The skin lit red and white and his eyes looked dark, like pitted fruit.

We hoped we'd be alone by the time we reached Devil's Den—who but us would think to be out there, all alone, on a Monday night?—but as we climbed the gravel roadway, we saw whole groups of people moving quietly among the rocks, shining their flashlights and clicking cameras.

"What are they doing?" I asked, incredulous.

"Ghost hunting, I think," Kevin said. "I've seen it before on television, but never before in person."

And for all the times I'd seen them—as a child, beside my parents—I'd never seen them in the grasses, only on sidewalks or by old, brick structures. They were looking for the ghosts of soldiers but looked like soldiers, themselves: thick clusters of men and women, moving slowly, quietly, carving patterns into the earth.

They came from everywhere, Kevin told me, citing a History Channel special—California, Florida, even Europe—to take photographs of floating orbs or the hazy figures just out of focus. And who, he asked, could blame them? For while tourists claimed they'd come to Gettysburg for the rocks, the fields, the observation towers, and the photos they could pose for at the top, what they really wanted to go home with was a story of something greater: how they witnessed something supernatural. How they came in contact with a ghost.

And here, they could say, pointing to a Polaroid, *is proof that they exist!*

From our seats on the dry, cracked hillside, they looked almost like shooting stars, their flashlights shining in one direction only long enough to catch our gaze.

"Look at them all," I said, and suddenly, for no reason, I wanted to cause a scene—to be loud and drunk and angry, jump from one boulder to the next, call to Kevin in the hot, white moonlight. Instead I watched them move, shadowy figures without faces.

"This is strange," I said at last.

"Definitely," Kevin said, again raising his flashlight to his face, and when he clicked the button on, I could see his veins bulge blue—an image that burned into my mind. "But what about the ghostsssss?" he said, laughing, and I hit him hard across the shoulder.

And then I think we split a roll of crackers, pulled up our hoods, and headed home.

That a brain can form new memories—phantom memories of events that never happened—is not altogether impossible, recent studies show. In a highly advertised and controversial 2013 study on the subjectivity and fabricated nature of memory, a team of scientists with the Center for Neural Circuit Genetics at the Massachusetts Institute of Technology presented evidence that proves memories can, in fact, be fabricated, then later recalled as vividly as if real.

The research, carried out on mice by scientists Susumu Tonegawa, Steve Ramirez, and Xu Liu, involved the gradual introduction of a subtle electric shock. The team first identified and chemically labeled the cluster of brain cells responsible for the formation of memory, then placed the mice in an environment where they were safe from electric shock. The following day, the team put them in another environment, this time administering the shock while simultaneously stimulating the previous day's memory cells. On the third day, the mice were reintroduced to their first environment, and as a result, they froze in anticipation—proof that a false memory had been produced, one that manifested in trepidation of an electric current that had never occurred.

The findings, the team reported, prove the unreliability of memory—in mice and, likely, humans. Their goal was quite simply to "make people realize even more than before how unreliable the human memory is." And that unreliability, Dr. Tonegawa reported, also prompts essential questions on the nature of evolution—chiefly, *Why is the human brain made in such a way that we can fabricate and form false memories?*

No one is certain, Dr. Tonegawa explained, but his own belief is that it has to do with creativity—that to ensure our own survival, humans must be capable of envisioning possible events and combinations of real and imagined occurrences in visceral and vivid detail.

"Unless you have that kind of ability," he said, "there is no civilization."

What's more, he argued, it's that rich and internal experience that fuels the most inspired work in the arts, the sciences, makes creative activities altogether possible. But it also provides proof that a possible "tradeoff for this tremendous benefit" is the remembrance, however pleasant or painful, of things that never even occurred.

Here's another memory I've perhaps written Kevin into: It's a warm night in Gettysburg, the spring of our sophomore year, and we're sitting Indian-style along the hardwood floor while our friend Leslie tells us about the ghosts.

"When I was a child," she says, "men and women climbed onto our porch at night to throw their bodies against the windows, or they lay flat along the floorboards, thumping their torsos against the wood. They pressed their hands to the glass, and they were always chanting, mumbling nonsense."

This was in Burkina Faso, West Africa, where for seven years Leslie lived with her parents. They were missionaries—tall, thin, bulblike people who remind us of librarians—and we've met them only once, on the first day of our sophomore year. They walked up and down the steps, carrying boxes of Leslie's stuff—African paintings and jars of spices, boxes of green tea and bamboo bowls—and because we knew these stories, we just looked at them and blinked.

In Africa, Leslie's father would yank the curtains, shout, usher his three small children into a single bedroom, where they were instructed to lock the door and wait. They propped a chair beneath the knob and then sat in utter darkness—"for hours sometimes," she tells us, "for however long it took"— with their bodies folded between two twin beds.

"Our father always herded us away so fast, but I remember just sitting there, listening to these complete strangers enter our living room, and you could hear them thrashing, but even worse was the sound of chinaware; my father would speak, *preach*, trying to get their ghosts or demons out, and they'd throw their bodies across the room and hit the cabinet where the plates were kept. We always just waited for it to stop."

She looks at her fingertips and squints, peeling beige polish from her nails. "And all I remember thinking is, *What am I going to do if they hurt my father?*"

I glance over at Kevin, who sits quietly along the wall, running his finger over his jeans and picking at a hole above his kneecap. "Wow," he says at last. "I can't imagine how scared I'd be."

"It was fine," Leslie says. "They never did, but I always worried."

Kevin and I cannot compete with Leslie's stories—they are difficult to even imagine. Our childhoods were only ever spent climbing oak trees and weeping willows, maybe a crab apple from time to time, but even then, the fruit was rotten. Leslie picked fresh mangoes and made guava-pulp lip balm with the security guard's only daughter.

"I wasn't supposed to hang out with her," she says, "but I did it, anyway."

Leslie tells us stories of elephants that once stopped traffic, a nine-foot snake her father shot in their backyard, a man who cooked his supper every night on the shell of a giant turtle— "He just sat on it, and it never moved," she says, "but we knew it was alive because later we'd see it grazing"—and how one time, in an African market, she was almost kidnapped by two grown men.

"One of them just picked me up," she says, "and started carrying me away. I don't remember it, of course; this is just a story I've been told. I was four, but our security guard—this big guy, obviously—tackled him, and the man just kept saying, 'I want to marry her, I want to make her my wife.' It was just because I was white—he'd never seen someone like me."

Through windows propped open with beer cans, we watch as a ghost tour moves along the sidewalk, the metal catching the glint of the ghost hunters' lanterns, the tourists peering in as they walk by. From his place along the dusty hardwood, Kevin opens a canister of loose tobacco and releases a pinch onto a rolling paper, folding it into a tight, long bundle before licking the ends to seal it shut.

"One more story," he says. "Then I want to have a smoke."

"Okay," Leslie says, sitting upright, thinking, her hands folded beneath her knees. "Okay, well, once, when my father was preaching in this small village at the end of town, the service ended and this man came up to us, which wasn't all that unusual, since people were always asking my father to pray for them: for their health, for the health of their loved ones. But this one man—his family brought him, this older couple and his wife. They said he needed to be saved, that he'd been roaming around the streets naked or whatever, drinking, not sleeping."

Kevin puts the cigarette on the floor and looks at her intently.

"So my dad puts his hands on the man's forehead and the man starts chanting," Leslie says. "Normally, my mother or the other church elders would try to escort us away since we were children, but no one thought of us that time, so we just stood there, watching, as this man began to shake—he did, he *shook*—and then his voice changed, and he started saying complete nonsense, words that weren't even words, and then his face, too, changed. And when my father finally got to 'In the name of Jesus Christ, I revoke you,' the man literally went flying—he flew backwards across the room, as if he'd been hit by an oncoming car."

We look at her, silent.

"And?" Kevin finally asks.

Leslie shrugs. "He just folded himself up, wormlike, and began to sob. He was completely back to his old self, his family said, except, of course, he was heaving."

Kevin stands and I lean forward. "Do you believe in demons?" I ask. "I mean, you lived there for seven years—do you believe it's even remotely possible? Ghosts or demons or whatever?"

Out the window, the tour moves closer, the guide's lantern swinging in the cool night air.

"The people that we met," Leslie says, "I can't see how they could make that up. It's part of their beliefs, sure, but to me it never felt fabricated. And it was horrifying as a child, you know, because of course you can't help but wonder: My dad prays these demons or ghosts or whatever out, but where do they go? Where do they go when they finally leave?"

The pain and suffering of the dead or dying, the psychic ringing that fails to cease.

"So I always thought," she says, sitting upright, "that they must go into us."

12

THE TRUTH IS, it doesn't matter if it was Kevin with me that night on those moonlit battlefields. It doesn't matter if it was him sitting in the living room with Leslie. It doesn't matter to me at all, because in the memory I replay most often—one I'm certain occurred with Kevin—we were standing in the up- stairs hallway of the Civil War reenactors' theme house, six- teen months before Emily's murder, and we were whispering to each other, laughing, rifling through open closets.

"Look at this," I said, pressing a hoopskirt to my waist.

Kevin wore a general's hat, like a top hat someone flat- tened. He adjusted the fit against his forehead and raised an empty copper cup. "I sure am thirsty," he said, squinting into an imaginary sun that was just a corner of the bedroom. "I sure am hungry," he said, rubbing his belly, and I laughed.

That house, in particular—and the students who inhabited it—had a role so intertwined with history it was hard to even imagine. To me, it was simply beautiful: a hundred-year-old white Victorian with sloping shutters and a bean-red door, but it had also been an inn, lodging soldiers and travelers just after the Civil War was won. Now it was student housing: three floors of hardwood lit by large, spacious windows, the rooms padded with bunk beds, small desks, and tall, wide armoires. It was a point of pride for our college, mentioned in brochures and on their website and, later, spotlighted by *The New York Times*, not because of the history within those walls, but because of the students who lived between them: men and women who woke early to reenact the Battle of Gettysburg on Saturday mornings. They dressed in vintage clothing, packed pocketknives and handkerchiefs, and while the women cooked beans in skillets, the men lay flat in fields. They had their battle movements memorized—each and every play—and spent their mornings waiting. They knew exactly when to die. And when at three they won the battle, they caravanned home together to park their van in our shared drive.

I was living there—though I did not want to—because every other building, theme houses and residential halls alike, were full, and there was nothing else. There was no other vacancy but in their home. The semester prior, I'd studied abroad, in Aix-en-Provence, France, and in its neighboring Mediterranean towns so small and quaint they looked like a cluster of tiny seashells from the vantage point of nearby mountains. I drank wine, ate pucks of soft-ripened cheese, jumped from a rocky cliff that jutted out above blue-green water while men in canvas hats pulled their lines from the darkest depths. But back in Gettysburg, Pennsylvania, Kevin filled a tub with water. He took the radios, stereos, and speakers from the bedrooms of his roommates, edged them along the rim, and prepared to enter. There was a candle burning on the bathroom countertop, and that's what Eric said was worse—that when he found our friend hunched over the bath's smooth rim, the light itself was moving, as if water.

"It looked wet along his body," Eric said. "I thought I was too late."

In their dimly lit, eerie bathroom, Eric convinced his college roommate to wrap himself in a cranberry towel. He pulled the cords from the nearby socket and then sat beside him against the tub. They waited like that for twenty minutes until health officials finally arrived.

"What did you two talk about?" I asked once, because to me those minutes seemed impossible—spaces reserved for situations I thought I'd never have to handle.

"For the most part, we were silent," Eric said. "We didn't talk about what happened, if that's what you want to know."

Kevin spent the five days that followed in the Reading Hospital, two hours east, talking to doctors and watching daytime television in a pair of sweatpants his mother had mailed him. The doctors diagnosed him with major depressive disorder—characterized by a pervasive pattern of depressive symptoms—and borderline personality disorder, which, among other things, causes "personal problems that induce extreme anxiety, distress, and depression." Then he returned to our college campus. By January, when I too returned, we stood there together in the reenactors' theme house—where I'd been assigned for the semester—and together, we raised our imaginary weapons and peered off into the distance.

"I've got the enemy in my sights," I said, and Kevin made a firing sound.

Outside, the world was quiet and brightly lit. It had snowed the night before, and the yard looked now like a Christmas card—like something carefully arranged as if to make my memory a little brighter. Autumn was long behind us, so we weren't talking about what had happened. We weren't talking about what he'd done. We were talking instead about the war— the thousands of men who gave their lives on the battlefields all around us, and how their ghosts were probably everywhere, rippling, colliding with the living.

"What if there's one in this very room?" Kevin said. "We wouldn't have any idea."

If it was history that was meant to matter, it was hard to remember as a resident. The house seemed, instead, a depository for the sorts of people I did not want to be associated with. Inside, students hung hoopskirts in shared closets and stored their muskets under beds. No one stole their canteens; no one filled them with vodka tonics. They were not confronted with jokes about their rucksacks or the purpose of their wineskins. In the house's only kitchen, they cooked nineteenth-century meals. They dried meat along the rooftop and hung their clothes on a line to dry. Sundays, they baked cornbread and broadcast fife music from iPod speakers.

I'd moved in and then grown distant, so that when they gathered for weekly dinners—salted meats and red-skin potatoes—and knocked gently on my door, I only ever turned their offers down.

"I've got a lot of work," I'd say, because it seemed best to remain an outsider: a strange and distant foreigner in their world.

I didn't hate the reenactors individually, but collectively, as a whole—their conversations and their wardrobes and the smells that followed them home: like campfire, and meat, and smoke. Kerosene and lighter fluid. Their faces were always charcoal-bruised and sweaty, and they tied their hair back in mousy braids. They even refused to use deodorant, citing a need for "authentic odors."

It was simple, at twenty-one, to think I had everything figured out. Emily was still alive, and Kevin, of course, had not yet killed her. The reenactors were my main concern, and I was better, I believed, for recognizing the futility in what they did. No matter how often they reenacted—no matter how fiercely they may have craved change—their outcome was predetermined; they could never escape their fate. Those who died would always die, and those granted life would have to live it, and always in the shadow—and the memory—of what had been lost.

For all of my resistance to their house and who they were, what's strangest to me now is that, in this memory, I was grateful. I was not upset but, frankly, pleased to be living inside their home. It was my first Saturday back on campus since my return to the United States and Kevin's discharge from the Reading Hospital, and the reenactors were out reenacting, fighting a war we could not see, so I told Kevin to come over to peek through dresser drawers and private closets.

"I bet they have the weirdest trinkets," I said, "antique viewfinders and vintage hats."

Kevin was a history major, and this is precisely why my new placement was so convenient—*It's exactly what he needs*, I thought, *to distract him from all that happened*. I had no experience addressing issues of mental illness or suicidal tendencies; it seemed beyond me even to try. So instead I attempted distraction, saying, *We'll have full rein of the entire house.*

"You can even be the Union," I joked. "I'll go unabashedly Confederate."

Kevin and I had been friends at that point for years, but still there seemed a limit on the type of conversations we could share. Mental illness was difficult, *heavy*, and we'd only ever talked about movies, music, the books we were reading and whether we thought they were any good, which, ironically, is what we'd do for years into his incarceration. In retrospect, however, Kevin's attempt at suicide was the only real warning sign something was ever wrong. Even the way in which I learned about his actions—even that felt strangely distant, the news arriving through an email sent by Eric marked with a small red iconic flag.

Kevin's not well, he wrote. *He's left campus to receive treatment.*

But I was four thousand miles away. The best that I could offer Kevin was a Hallmark card in a foreign language with a phrase he wouldn't even understand. *Je suis désolée*, or some photo of purple flowers. It would cross the country and then an ocean to arrive in the States pitifully late.

Okay, I wrote back. *Let me know as things progress.*

It seemed strange to me that Kevin was suffering so intensely, so invisibly, so quietly, without any of us knowing, but strangest of all was a gift I'd purchased for him that evening in the Christmas market in the *rotonde*. I'd spent my night purchasing chocolates and packs of note cards, boxes of almond-shaped candies called *calissons*, but for my closest friends in Gettysburg, I'd bought small bars of homemade soap—clunky blocks shaped smooth and round by the hands of perfect strangers. They were scented with herbs and peels of fruit, and they were cheap and European. They seemed an easy gift to buy. Just a simple French trinket, something my friends would tease me about, but like.

And yet it seemed strange and coincidental that of all the things to buy I'd chosen the gift of a bath accessory. And if I gave that gift to Kevin, I wondered, would it remind him of what he had done? Would it remind him of that desire? Would he know they told me, too?

And in that moment when Eric found him—when he saw Kevin's body stretching across the tub—was there a second where he lingered? Unsure how to tell our friend he shouldn't do it? That life would soon get better? That all he needed was to wait and see?

And after everything that's happened, I wonder now if he'd still say it.

It was the distance, I tell myself when I need to. *That's really what's to blame.*

But in truth, I never asked Kevin how he felt for fear it was an inappropriate question. Even when I returned to campus—when I finally finished setting up my room—I avoided him for days. When finally I invited him over, he must have known how strange I felt; he stood holding a thermos of coffee and his gaze was on his shoes.

"I got us blueberry bagels," he said. "I know you like them best."

Miles away, the reenactors lay still in snowy grass, so I propped open their heavy door, gesturing for Kevin to come inside. "Please," I said. "Join me," and I bowed as he passed me by.

They had this coming is what I thought—these grown men who spent their mornings in barren fields, like children playing make-believe. They were strange, and awkward, and oafish, their faces pocked with acne scars, and they smelled like something sour: like dough rising in a bowl. I hated who they were and how I'd been placed right there beside them, so what else could I do but make fun of the way they lived? I didn't feel bad pulling apart their dressers, or pushing their hangers from side to side.

In the room just off the parlor, I held up a lacy bonnet, a sweat stain permeating its inner rim. "Look," I said to Kevin, pulling it down over my ears.

"Be sure to put that back," he said. "I bet this stuff's expensive."

In the kitchen, I made us coffee while Kevin walked slowly down their hallway, running his fingers first over doorframes and then each small bronze rectangular sign. I could hear him over the running water—"This one charged Seminary Ridge," he said. "This one fought at Devil's Den"—and I leaned out into the hallway, calling back to him.

"Each room is dedicated to a key Civil War player," I said. "You can see which by a placard outside each door."

And while the house featured the Buford Room and the Hooker Room and the Meade Room and more, I'd been gifted the Abraham Lincoln bedroom, easily the nicest in the house. It was gigantic, with a boxy corner for a desk and two padded big bay windows. Morning light poured through twin oak trees and shined liquid across the floorboards, and it was tucked quietly in the back, with a separate entrance and a private, spacious bathroom.

"This is so incredible," Kevin said. "I wanted to live here, but never did."

"So pretend you do for now," I said, leading him up their staircase. He walked beside me, solemn, quiet, but when we reached General Lee's Headquarters—a cramped, one-person alcove with a slanted ceiling and a small, round window—he looked at me expectantly, unsure how exactly to proceed.

I walked over and turned the knob.

From the window, we could see all of Gettysburg: the buildings and streets and shops, and beyond, the observation towers and all those fields. They were white and soft and shining, glittering like glass beneath the sun.

"This is great," he said excitedly, and I felt suddenly proud to stand beside him.

He's not wishing for his death, I thought, *but the vivacity of his future.*

"The Confederates moved that way," he said, dragging his finger through the clean, clear air. "They moved in dense formation until they reached the rocks of Devil's Den."

He said it and I tried to picture them, take interest the way he did. I pictured men and then whole armies, soldiers hidden among the rocks. I saw clusters of young, tan man clutching rifles, their foreheads hot. I saw them crouching low, their bodies hiding among the brush, while women waited in clapboard houses, their children clinging to nightgown hems.

The bayonet I remember plainly. It was a replica, likely plastic, and leaned against the farthest corner, propped up neatly against the wall. When Kevin held it in his hands, his face turned tight in exhilaration.

"*Cool,*" he said softly, as if any loudness would make the bayonet fade. He laughed and then lunged forward, pretending to stab me in the chest.

"You've got me!" I said, falling, and when I rose, we ate our bagels.

We explored the house for another hour, and then Kevin left and I forgot: about his hospitalization, his depression, any responsibility I had to him as his friend. I let the days turn into weeks and those weeks turn into months. An entire year went by, and we cooked dinners and went to movies, hung out with friends and drank cheap beer, but never—in all that time—did I ask Kevin how he'd felt, or how it was that he felt now.

I kept his bar of soap in a drawer inside my desk.

When the following autumn he began to date Emily Silverstein, I was happy for him. She brought him out of himself, he said. She talked about things that truly mattered.

"It's like I completely open up," he said. "I can tell her anything."

I knew precisely what he meant, but again there was that discomfort. Mental illness seemed too taboo, too intimate a conversation to share between two friends; it seemed some secret, private burden, one I—and many others—thought he could carry on his own.

It was only after Kevin's crime and then his sentencing and then, eventually, his relocation that I acquired and then reviewed the public records as sent to me by the receptionist at the Adams County Courthouse. I knew, of course, they would be difficult. There were mental health evaluations and inventories of evidence, Emily's autopsy, and testimonials. There were search warrants and detailed descriptions and letters attesting to unbearable grief. But it was through these files I also learned that Kevin had been trying to take his own life that night. Emily had tried to stop him.

"She was exhausted and run-down," her friends stated to police. "She was the only one talking to Kevin," or perhaps the only one he felt he could talk to, "but she couldn't take it anymore."

They should take a break, Emily suggested, until the situation improved.

This is when he went into the kitchen to find a knife, a psychiatrist noted during an evaluation. *He states he was not angry at Emily and did not have homicidal urges toward her. He said he had only a wish to die.*

Emily began pleading—"Kevin, please. Kevin, stop"—and when he raised the blade to his thin, white skin, she lunged forward in an attempt to grab it.

This is where Kevin's memory becomes fuzzy, the psychiatrist wrote. *Kevin reported pushing her back and somehow he wound up on top of her and began stabbing her in the neck.*

It happened instantly, and after he came to, Kevin tried desperately to revive her: first tying fabric around her wounds in an attempt to alleviate the loss of blood, then finally carrying her to the tub, thinking at least he could contain it. He sat beside her for twenty minutes, crying, before finally phoning the Gettysburg police, and when asked why he didn't take his own life—if that was really what he meant to do—he told police, very simply, "I didn't mean to hurt her."

He said, "It was *my* life I wanted to take."

In a statement read the day of his sentencing, he apologized to her parents, to his parents, to everyone.

I've been suffering and grieving each and every day for her, he wrote. *And I will spend the rest of my life doing all the good I can possibly do.*

It's not a memory, but I can picture it: I see my friend sitting in the Gettysburg jail on the night of his arrest, his hands folded across his lap, grown men standing all around him. His wrists are bound in handcuffs, his eyes are red and raw. It isn't difficult to envision, and there is paperwork to back it up: evidence and crime scene notes and not one but three mental health evaluations that all attest to what Kevin claims: that he wanted to end his own life, that he needed a break from the pain he felt.

It is my professional opinion, one reads, *that Mr. Schaeffer demonstrated signs of impaired functioning prior to and at the time of the offense, and therefore lacked the capacity to comprehend the wrongfulness of his actions and conform his behaviors to the requirements of the law.*

Kevin was unclear as to what he was doing or why he was doing it, reads another, *but I believe he had no thought of ever killing Emily.*

And finally, there is this: *This is truly a tragic case.*

I replay that sunlit, winter memory now and I'm always looking for something new: a detail I never noticed, a way to make the ending change. It's almost as if I can will it into existence—that, if I want it bad enough, I have the power to rewrite everything: to turn to Kevin in that upstairs bedroom and say, "I am someone you can talk to," say, "I am here for you."

"I've never done that," I might have said, "but I understand how someone could."

How, sometimes, life feels hard. How maybe it's only normal not to want it.

"This is something we can talk about," or "We don't have to keep this quiet."

Instead, I said nothing and now I wonder. For the many moments that have escaped me, I still recall that morning with exactitude: the snow, the smell of coffee, my friend standing, youthful, in the hall. The first time I'd seen him since his hospitalization, and already I wanted to sweep it under the rug.

In a letter he'd eventually write from Albion, he'd inquired why this was.

It's not like you're to blame, of course, he wrote, *but I sort of felt like a leper—all those months, I couldn't understand why you all acted like nothing had happened.*

I replay that morning often, but each time I'm reenacting, attempting revision, and always failing. I hold up a fraying hoopskirt, pull the vintage fabric over my jeans.

"Look," I say to Kevin, spinning, pretending I'm a ballerina. "A Civil War ballerina," I say, and I hold the fabric to my hips and move.

13

FOR AS COMPLICATED AS IT MAY BE, my reaction to suicide now is the same as when I first encountered it—as an eleven-year-old, when my brother's friend Robby put a rag in the exhaust pipe of his family's station wagon, turned on Nirvana, and faded out.

This is how we referred to it, my brother and me. I was eleven and Wesley was thirteen, and we didn't know any better than to say Robby had simply "faded out."

We were still sufficiently children.

The details surrounding Robby's suicide remain largely ambiguous, even to this day, though it was rumored his parents were in the midst of a bitter divorce, and it was possible that Robby was gay and therefore bullied in our small town. But what everyone knew with certainty—what was repeated, again and again—was the way Robby took his life: by listening to Nirvana's *Nevermind* once, maybe twice, and then fading out completely. His mother discovered him in the garage, we were told—for god knows what reason—and as a child, I imagined her holding a bag of groceries, saw the milk jug drop and spill, the liquid spreading across the concrete, and it's now that image I remember most.

Because we were scared to know so many answers, my brother and I didn't ask a lot of questions. It seemed like an illness, pure and simple.

This, we decided, was what happened if you were sick in all the wrong ways, or if you were sick and no one knew. Of course I obsessed daily about how one could avoid that particular illness, as invisible as the wind—imagined it slipping into his pores, his lungs and brain the way sleep overtakes a body.

And for years, it was enough: the idea that Robby got sick and it overtook him.

Years later, in my late teens, I would rebel against this notion. Depression was no excuse, I decided, suicide no solution.

But I realize now that the pain that Kevin felt—that night, and for the nearly eighteen months beforehand, since his suicide attempt—was no less real, no less urgent, than a heart attack, a stroke, a seizure. Than the sensation of running too hard or running too fast, keeling over, gasping for air. Wishing for something to fill your lungs—to rush in and then revive you—except nothing ever does, and maybe nothing ever can.

It is unpleasant, of course, to sympathize with suicide. It is unpleasant to believe in a reality in which death is the only option. And it is problematic, certainly, to compare suicide to running, to cardiac arrest, to terminal cancer. But this is precisely the problem: There is no fair parallel that can be drawn between those who have felt the dark pull of suicide and those who never have.

In his 2012 op-ed on the suicide of famed film director Tony Scott, mental health expert Dr. Charles Raison writes that severe mental depression is "probably the most unbearable pain a human being can withstand for any protracted period of time. Many people who died of cancer have written eloquently about how the crushing pain from their tumors paled in comparison to the pain they felt when depressed. With all other pain, most people can maintain some sense of separation between themselves and the pain. As horrible as it is, the pain is in their arm, or leg, or belly or head. But there is still a 'them' that is separate from the misery. Depression is different. Because it is at its essence a perceptual disorder, it causes one to see the entire world as pain. It feels painful inside, but it also feels painful outside.

"When a person is depressed," Dr. Raison continues, "the entire world is disturbed and distressed, so there is nowhere to escape."

I understand that pain, too, because I was once consumed by it. I was thirteen, a child who still wore pajamas printed with the faces of New England wildlife—MAKE THE MOOSE OUT OF LIFE, they read—and yet every night when I wore them to bed, it was death I wanted most, lying still in that silent darkness.

I'd think, *I wish that it would find me.*

Even now, even all these years later, I've no rational explanation for that desire or the urgency I felt—a pull so strong it often compelled me to sit in my parents' closet and touch the barrel of my father's rifle, propped innocuously in a corner between his tackle box and a row of shoes. I liked to run my fingers over its cool exterior and dare myself to touch it: the small metal trigger, which seemed frightening despite its size.

But I never picked it up. I knew even then that to pick up that rifle would be to enter a territory I had no faith I could explore carefully.

It was likely chemical, a friend would later tell me. We were sitting in my apartment in Iowa, the lights from passing cars shining iridescently across our faces. I'd admitted to her my young obsession after too much wine and whiskey. There were ten years and a thousand miles separating me from my own young, suicidal self, but it felt closer to me than ever.

"Your body was just going through puberty," she said. "It was probably that chemical imbalance that set you off."

Chemical imbalance. I think about these words now the way I think about fate, or love, or happiness, though often fate seems more real to me now than the latter two ever could. Yet, they all conjure abstract notions that instill fear and raw excitement—the idea of the unknowable, in all its flawed and mysterious glory. In truth, I'm not even certain now that the gun my father owned would have worked even if I'd tried. I once asked him, feigning interest in family heirlooms, curious only to know if what I'd thought so long about could have ever even truly happened—if I could have ended my life right then, at thirteen, *as a child*.

"I don't think so," he said, distracted. It was just an antique, he said, a gift from his own father. He'd held on to it for its sentimentality. He didn't think he'd ever even fired it.

"The dust alone would've probably clogged it," he joked, buttering a piece of toast.

Still, broken or not, nothing changes what I recall: the strange and foreign sensation of crossing the front lawn every afternoon, wiping my sneakers along the mat, and then retreating to their upstairs bedroom to sit, entranced, beside the weapon on their well-worn, sea-foam-green carpet, trying to will myself to do it.

Go on. Just pick it up.

It wasn't the gun's violence I wanted most—that much remains unambiguous. And it wasn't the reverberations of pain or heartache, or some unspoken attempt at belated parental attention. What I wanted was simply this: for my life to end very quietly, very subtly, without any immediate or long-lasting repercussion to the ones I loved the most.

My dog, my parents, my brothers. My betta fish, Allen Iverson.

I had no motive, no causation, for that sadness, and the peer pressure and bullying I experienced was no greater, as far as I can tell, than anyone else's I've ever met. There was just some profound unsettlement with my life, and I'd acquired an interest in ending it.

I sat for hours at a time in that closet that smelled like feet and dirty laundry, but I could never bring myself to do it. There was always an image I could not ignore: my mother sunning herself on the dock of the lake house where we spent our summers, my father casting out his fishing line, my brothers arguing over an inner tube as our dog yapped at tiny fish that swam in circles around her paws. I could not shake my place there beside them—on a towel, unfurled and wet. That image demanded my presence. That landscape was where I belonged.

When school ended in June, my mother took me with her on a class trip to Rome and Paris, as if she knew I needed a change. These excursions were ones she did often—acting as a chaperone to her thirty high school French students on ten-day field trips that involved long hours on European buses with their boxy TVs and neon seats—and I spent those days beside her, looking in the windows of every storefront, imagining my life within their cities. It was that trip that likely saved me. While sitting on that tour bus on a bridge high above the Seine, I remember most just looking down—fleetingly, at the blue-green water—and watching as rows of people passed beneath us on slow-moving boats. It came to me almost instantly: *This is worth everything.*

That life is worth *every* moment, however good, however bad.

Somehow, understanding that this world was a part of my own—and seeing it with my own eyes—pulled me out of myself. It was every bit as simple as it sounds: a switch that, somehow, flipped.

And what remains upsetting now, most of all, is not that very desperate and urgent way I felt—which, above all, seemed a deprivation of some essential life force, something as vital as calories, or water, or air—but that this was the pain Kevin likely felt for months, for over a year, until finally it peaked on that April night. And I knew it, and I had known it, and still I was silent, and I'd said nothing.

Perhaps if the pain of suicide had never been accessible to me, I would find Kevin's actions—and the impulse that initially drove them—easier to forget. Probably, I would. I would not still be in communication with him, for example, and certainly not obsessing over what he did. It's unlikely I'd have spent a hundred dollars and countless hours acquiring photocopies of the entire criminal case compiled against him, and they would not sit in—weigh down—my desk drawer. Of that I'm almost certain.

In all likelihood, I would never travel to Albion in the first place, if not for a quick gas-up along the highway or a trip to use the McDonald's restroom. But perhaps I find myself obsessed because I understand the difficult experience of simply existing; I have been there and know it well. And my obsession, then, is borne not of fascination, but by complete and absolute failure. By the fact that, for as much as I hate suicide, I also understand it.

I wish, of course, this wasn't true. I wish I hated suicide and hated more those capable of it, found them to be inherently selfish individuals, cheaters of life and struggle and hardship, felt they were taking the easy way out—a shortcut, if you will—although that is exactly what it is, I suppose: a way to get somewhere faster.

. . .

But the truth is that I believe in the possibility of unendurable, insufferable sadness. I believe in a pain so real, so raw, it could be made visible, a shining bulb that burns us whole. A wound that yields such intense pain that death may well seem the only reprieve. I believe this because, for months after I learned what happened—Emily lunging at Kevin desperately in an attempt to free the knife—I studied the effects of severe depression, the symptoms of abrupt withdrawal from antidepressants, the way perception shifts as a result of suicidal ideation.

For those in pain, suicide, however awful, offers a quicker, more definite solution. The outcome is predetermined, assuming the method is efficient, and those who pursue this option often think others, too, will be better off without them. Unlike therapy, or medicine, or regular appointments with specialists whom insurance companies may or may not cover, death is absolute, and therefore it is alluring.

The alternative much less so. Resolution, of course, takes time, and in the most recent statistic compiled on the issue, officials revealed that it takes the average American eight years to seek professional treatment for mental illness; in that time, nearly three percent attempt suicide at least once, though many more than once. Worse even still, it is estimated that one to two percent of all suicides involve the killing of an additional person or, in many cases, multiple individuals.

I cannot say—because I was not there, because I could never be in another's head, much less a man's just prior to murder—what factors, specifically, drove Kevin to kill Emily.

I like to think—though I do not know—he had no control over his decision. But I do believe Kevin did not want to talk about his feelings for the same reasons I never did; we were ashamed of having them in the first place.

And yet how prevalent they are. According to a recent study, it was determined that depression is the leading cause of disability in the United States, and in 2013, it was determined the leading cause of death, surpassing even car accidents, which killed 33,687 that year.

Suicide claimed the lives of 38,364.

By 2030, the World Health Organization projects, depression will be the leading cause of global disability, resulting not only in huge economic and social costs, but also in a substantial decrease in the quality of life for millions of Americans.

And as a result of ongoing budget cuts, states are increasingly neglecting the needs of the mentally ill. In April of 2013, for example, Maryland revoked $7.2 million in funding for mental health services.

"Wishing that mental illness would not exist," former American Psychiatric Association president Paul Appelbaum told a crowd of supporters during his inaugural address, "has led our policymakers to shape a health care system as if it did not exist."

Do I believe we can be haunted, in some way, by sadness? I do.

I believe it even when I know that thousands have received effective treatment, that thousands are now happy and healthy and vibrant, beautifully broken and full of life. They marry and live in the countryside and write charming notes to their partner that they later leave beside the kitchen sink.

I love you, and help yourself to some cake!

But this is to say nothing of the thousands who remain unwell, or who remain undiagnosed and untreated entirely. According to a 2012 survey published by the Substance Abuse and Mental Health Services Administration, over twenty percent of Americans report having some form of mental illness. Forty-six percent of people, reports the *New England Journal of Medicine*, believe those who suffer from mental illness are far more dangerous than others. Seventy-one percent of respondents claimed they wouldn't want to work closely with someone suffering from mental illness, and sixty-seven percent said they wouldn't want a neighbor with a mental illness.

"People want to believe that the problem is easy to solve, and that they can somehow insulate themselves from the risks of . . . violence by insulating themselves from people with mental illness," reports Steven Hoge, a psychiatry professor at Columbia University. But "it is virtually impossible to identify who among the mentally ill are likely to be violent."

In fact, even psychiatrists have a difficult time predicting when a patient is at a heightened risk for violence or suicide, because those who truly want to kill themselves often stay silent and simply do it. Suicide, Hoge writes, is often "an impulsive act driven by acute and unpredictable increases in anxiety and despair that one cannot predict in advance."

But most important and above all, he writes, it is undeniably untrue that talking about suicide increases the likelihood that it will happen, most especially in youths.

In fact, studies suggest just the opposite, he writes.

And so while our friends might envision aggression—an anger as sharp as the weapon he held—it is difficult for me to imagine Kevin in that moment as anything but profoundly sad, lost irretrievably inside himself. I am an adult but I am also five, watching television with my mother, wondering what it is that caused my friend's mind to break.

14

I AM NOT A PROFESSIONAL RESEARCHER, not a psychologist, not a trained specialist or social activist. I am no one, really. But even someone who is no one can see that our country faces a problem—that we stand at the precipice of an all-afflicting epidemic, one that manifests in myriad ways, often violent, and unforeseen.

Even now, even all these years later, I turn on the television to a row of squad cars outside a building, men hunched low over matte and metallic roofs, and feel the familiar pull that is that violence, animalistic, just out of sight. I watch another shooting at a school, grocery store, mall, theater, or gym flicker across the evening news, and I have to remind myself of what I know is true: that however similar in ideology, their violence is not the same. Kevin did not walk into an elementary school and shoot children, of course, one by one. There are many, *many* differences. But for all intents and purposes, what happened to these men is the same: They were sick, and no one knew.

But how, exactly, does that shift occur? How does a person whose pain has always been internalized transition abruptly, feel the need to externalize it? In my exhaustive search for answers, I've read everything I can—attempts, however feeble, to understand the transformation that occurred in Kevin, and in Jared Loughner, and in James Holmes, and in Adam Lanza, or in any other mind that thinks to instigate an act of terrible violence.

Compelling arguments exist about these crimes of absolute brutality—theories that argue violence as a marker of masculinity, or violence as the result of an absence of strong male role models, or that male privilege is inferred inherently and, when denied, cause for psychic chaos. There is no denying the simple figures, the solitary denominator shared by these events: how ninety-five percent of all violent crimes in America are perpetrated by men.

There have been thirty-one mass school shootings in this nation between 1996 and the time of this writing; all thirty-one were committed by men. All but one of sixty-four public massacres were also committed by men—a trend that recalls perhaps most vividly when Seung-Hui Cho, twenty-three, who on April 16, 2007, stormed Virginia Tech in Blacksburg, gunning down thirty-two people in two campus locations and wounding seventeen others before eventually committing suicide.

Adam Lanza, twenty, took the lives of twenty-seven students

and faculty members on December 14, 2012, at Sandy Hook Elementary School in Newtown, Connecticut.

George Hennard, thirty-five, crashed his pickup into a Killeen, Texas, cafeteria and then abruptly opened fire, taking the lives of twenty-two people on October 16, 1991.

James Huberty, forty-one, used a pump-action shotgun, a handgun, and a semiautomatic rifle to kill twenty-one adults and children at a California McDonald's on July 18, 1984.

Charles Joseph Whitman, twenty-five, shot and killed sixteen students and faculty members on the University of Texas campus on August 1, 1966, after first taking the lives of his mother and wife.

Jiverly Wong took the lives of thirteen people on April 3, 2009, in Binghamton, New York, and months later, on November 5, 2009, so too did Nidal Malik Hasan in Fort Hood, Texas.

The list goes on to include George Banks and Aaron Alexis, Mark Barton and Michael McLendon. Mark James Robert Essex, Scott Evans Dekraai, and Omar Thornton. Christopher Speight and Robert Stewart, Robert Hawkins and Jeff Weise.

Gian Luigi Ferri. Joseph Wesbecker. Michael Silka. Carl Robert Brown.

We can trace the history all we want, but the bigger concern is this: What is it about our nation that inspires our men to kill?

Robert Bly, poet, activist, and leader of the mythopoetic men's movement, offers what I feel is the most compelling argument, one I'm certain is true of Kevin. Shame, Bly states in an interview with PBS, and what he deems "a lack of expressiveness in men," have led to profound emotional damage and is at the root of our epidemic of male violence.

Men take in a tremendous amount of shame, he argues, and while women also take in shame, they are socially encouraged to talk about it. By way of example, Bly explains the way a man and a woman externalize their pain; whereas a woman may kick a garbage can in anger or frustration, then phone a friend to discuss the underlying stressor, a man instead ignores his stress.

"[He doesn't] even think of it until two or three in the afternoon, when [he gets] home and suddenly—bam—it comes out . . . Expressiveness means that you continue to do it, you don't wait until two in the afternoon," Bly argues.

Or, for that matter, I thought, *four o'clock in the morning.*

It is all too easy, when drawing comparisons, to put one truth beside another and assume that they are equal. For so long, I wanted to draw parallels which, at first, were very flawed. An uncanny comfort arises from the thought of something complex as instead being quite simple, undiluted, boiled down. And it is helpful, when working through a trauma, to group yourself as part of a bigger movement, evidence that your struggle is just one of many.

But it seems clear to me now that a man coming off antidepressants—a man proven to be experiencing a dissociative state, a man who had tried to commit suicide in that state and instead mistakenly killed his intervening girlfriend—is an altogether different man from the ones on the evening news. Those men spend weeks, months, often even years methodically planning the murders of many strangers. Neither their maleness nor their mental illness is a similar enough factor to make my friend an Adam Lanza.

It is a very flawed way of thinking.

But what I do know is this: Our nation faces a call to provide emotionally and mentally for our men. Kevin's crime, in other words, may be a result of his own reluctance, but also the reluctance of those around him. And while he'll spend most of his life in prison—receiving parole at forty-nine if he is lucky, or seventy-seven if he is not—it is ludicrous for anyone to believe that the problem of mental illness can be deterred by a prison sentence.

At present, the United States currently has the highest documented incarceration rate in the world, at 754 per 100,000. Of these, 2,225 prisoners are serving life sentences without parole for crimes that they committed while they were still juveniles. There are three times as many mentally ill people in jails as in hospitals, and the rate of mental illness in the prison system is five times that of the general population. And because, upon their release, inmates are not provided adequate aid—mental, emotional, and physical support—the current rate of recidivism demonstrates that a staggering one-third of all released inmates find themselves back inside within the year. Within three years, that number doubles.

As Americans, we want, naively, to believe this has to do with the failure of individuals, when it is actually the failure of our reentry, parole, and prison systems. In her 2013 book

Among Murderers: Life After Prison, author Sabine Heinlein writes, "In terms of empathy, murderers are obviously very low (if not lowest) on our list of priorities." In preparation for her book, Heinlein spent more than two years interviewing residents of a prominent halfway house in West Harlem, residents responsible for taking other people's lives. Her subjects had recently been released after serving several decades in prison, and Heinlein carefully documented the challenges the men encountered on their journey to freedom. Besides the everyday tasks of general living—finding work and forging relationships and, eventually, forgiving themselves—the men struggled with learning to live with their remorse among society's ever-present thirst for vengeance.

Violent crime is a lifelong sentence, she explains, even if those convicted are granted parole. And to be a prisoner is not only to face a sentence, but to absorb it as a way of life, as a forever constant component to identity.

"Rehabilitative programs are virtually absent in prison," she says. "To make people 'better,' we have to assess and treat them on an individual basis. Otherwise it's a cruel, irresponsible, costly, and ineffective process. The system is in need of reform. Rehabilitation is a very complex issue, and with the masses of people we keep behind bars, it's something we're obligated to think about."

To be inside a prison, in other words, is to understand firsthand the difficulties those men will later face, even regardless of their mental health. Of course, we don't like to think this way. We like, above all, to believe this: that we have power over our thoughts and actions. Even in imagining the brain, we picture it as iconic: the illustration always gray and gauzy, looping, a rounded amassing of unassuming mush.

But I think of the brain now and it's not that image I once imagined. I picture apartment buildings—poorly constructed and impossibly built. I picture homes stacked above other homes, people cooking omelets on broken burners, heaters plugged in and oscillating. Most days, the residents of these homes live peacefully with one another—they take showers, sing songs, and watch television—but one day, an oven's left on, or someone forgets to unplug the iron. Or maybe that's not it, either—maybe the people have nothing to do with it at all. But still come these chemical explosions, far too small and too complex to see, sending red and sparking embers into the drywall of our minds.

"Fire!" we say. "Fire!" But still we stand there and watch it burn.

15

WHEN AT LAST MY NAME IS CALLED, I walk through the metal detector, holding my breath. Everything slows, dulls, the world foggy as if I've gone feverish, or as if I'm moving underwater. I hand the woman at the desk my roll of quarters, and she carefully inspects the paper lining before breaking the roll in half and running her fingers over the smooth gray coins.

"Okay," she says, satisfied there's no powder glued between them, but I have no idea what happens next.

"That door?" I ask, pointing. On either side are buttons: SECURE ACCESS, one reads, and THIS AREA MONITORED BY VIDEO SURVEILLANCE.

"Hit the button farthest left," she says, pressing a stamp to my thin, white skin, but when I hold up my hand to inspect it, nothing appears in the place she's pressed.

The door buzzes and then clicks, and when I pull the heavy handle, I see a hallway like in the movies: long and white and narrow, lined entirely by slabs of glass. Beyond, I can make out a flattened patch of grass with a beat-up, splintered picnic table. Kevin politely calls it the "courtyard."

We get an hour out there to socialize, he wrote once, but it is yellow and dry and terse, a dismal place at best.

I press another button, and from a small intercom speaker, a man asks my name and the name of the inmate I am visiting. When I tell him—"Kevin Schaeffer"—the doors swoosh open to reveal another desk, this one enclosed entirely in glass.

"Stamp?" a man asks. I raise my hand to a small infrared light where a *B* glows in blue. *Why B?* I think to ask, but he is not here to answer my questions. He is here with a gun and a Taser, watching me as I move.

But even more disconcerting is the visitation room that looms beyond: eight round tables with four chairs each, a few bucket seats, and a big front desk. There will be no glass this time, between us, as there was when I visited him in Gettysburg while he awaited trial. No telephone or countertop. Our only border is four white walls adorned with pastel paintings of religious scenes: a man accepting a loaf of bread, a man riding horseback through a lush, green forest. Beneath, a row of vending machines blink with color, their tiered snacks and sodas like game show prizes.

At this point, Kevin wrote, *you'll have to be patient and wait.*

And this waiting would be hard, he said, because this wait would take some time. As a way of deterring riots, the inmates are led out individually, rather than en masse, their hands cuffed until they are released to the loved ones waiting who have come to secure their freedom, however temporarily. Across the room, the woman in heavy makeup places her hand on the wrist of her beloved and no one seems to care. I watch as children are lifted into the big, orange arms of their fathers, as couples embrace in quick, limp hugs. Beyond them, in the corner, I spot a girl who looks my age wearing Uggs and gray sweatpants, a black T-shirt that reads GO STATE, and I smile when I see her, decide she is just like me.

We are good to them for doing this, I think. *We know exactly what friendship means.* But when an older man walks toward her, she hugs him to her chest in a way that suggests he is her father.

Try to secure Scrabble, Kevin wrote, so I make my way to the front desk. His implication was that the game was popular, coveted, one of the first to get snatched up, so the sets might be scattered, the boards ripped from repeated folding, the tiles lost. With just a few hours each month to visit, the game's integrity is likely not a priority for the inmates, but for me, it is essential, and if anyone is to do the snatching here, it absolutely must be me, because I have no idea if—off the page—Kevin and I can still converse, and if I get stuck on what to say—if I get scared and begin to panic—I want to have these tiles: these squares of smooth brown wood. I want to pretend I'm only thinking, that I'm strategizing my next move. I'm formulating words, planning *pottery*, or *otter*.

At the cart beside the desk, I find a board game and a sack of letters, and while there are far fewer than expected, there are enough to make some words. I move the tiles across the board, glancing up idly at the doors. *Friend*, I spell out simply, as if this alone could be enough. As if—with only language—I can remember what matters most.

I am trying to imagine—as I have now for many months—how it will feel to finally see him. To feel his presence within close proximity. The very existence of our friendship has long been dependent upon the very fact of his incarceration; its terms were of great comfort. Writing allowed me to remain oblivious to his daily horrors, his daily world—I could imagine the food, the solitude, the fear, but without ever having to know its shape or exact specifics.

I knew from childhood that anything of value—a porcelain bowl, an animal—had to be cared for and loved entirely, its value dependent upon its daily maintenance, but when it came to Kevin, I'd valued my own comfort above all else. I wanted to shine a light into his life without stepping into what I knew was his daily darkness.

Even now, it's hard to say what I find most troubling—Kevin's quiet or my desire for distance. Both of us, it's clear, are searching for understanding. We both suffer from a lack of peace. Our minds are playing tricks on us with what we fail to comprehend.

Whether or not there's ever any progress—it remains difficult to say.

Still, I find myself wondering often about the idea of life as narrative. My whole childhood, I'd believed our lives were stories—that, from an early age, every choice we made was a plot point, our friends and family our main characters.

Everything we did—every moment of existence—could be condensed into a single sentence: I came, I saw, I conquered, I did something, I died.

Everyone had a story, and they were all very similar: We were on a journey, and so we made it or we didn't. We were happy or we weren't. We were rich or we were not. We did something, or we made something, or we produced nothing at all. But no matter how you told it, our stories still were stories.

But I wonder now how our stories can change. How they may take shape without us even knowing.

I thought to drive to Albion and see him would provide a sense of closure, help me make sense of Emily's death, but sitting inside his prison, watching the door, moving the tiles, I began to wonder about alternative endings. I began to wonder about character depth. How one simple event could make a life story change.

Does it matter, I've often wondered, *if I was drunk that April night?*

Does it matter if it was me who phoned him, who said, "Let's drink"? Does it make me an accomplice, however small, or responsible, a source of blame?

Does my youth count for anything? My naiveté at twenty-two?

Or what if that's not it, either? How might the story have changed if I'd been sober when I said goodnight? If I'd thought to inquire about him? If I'd told him of my ongoing experience of depression, of my suicidal ideation, that secret shame I'd long repressed? The gun leaning against the closet corner and how badly I'd once wanted it to go off?

I suppose what I really want to know is this: Would Emily still be alive if I'd suggested we go for pizza that night, instead?

When finally Kevin emerges, I am surprised how similar he looks; for the many ways our lives have changed, he himself has stayed the same, if a little older, a little stronger, and there is comfort—and joy—in that. I've spent months trying to determine how I would feel inside this moment, and yet I find myself responding as if by instinct, pressing him against my chest, feeling his collarbone against my own. I place my hands across his shoulders.

"Kevin," I say. "Kevin. It's so good to see you. It's been so long."

"Yeah," he says. He shrugs. Then: "It has, it has, it has."

His eyes are nervous as they watch me, as if awaiting some sudden movement. For however conflicted my mind might be, my own body is fluid with affection. I reach out and touch his arm. "Really," I say. "Really. I'm really happy to finally be here."

"It's good to see you," he says, and in this moment, I feel the same. We take our seats at the small, round table and I try to think of something smart to say, words that will set fire to this reunion, but I can only think to ask him questions.

"How are you?" I ask.

"Fine," he says. "As good as can be expected."

Then he tells me about his life—the twenty hours he works weekly in the prison's library, how he's begun reading his three hundredth book. "*The Collected Dialogues of Plato*," he says. "I like 'Euthydemus' best."

"Are you serious?" I say. "I can't imagine Plato as pleasure reading."

"There's a lot of time," he tells me slowly.

In this moment, I can see myself weeks from now, sitting on my couch so far away, the hard part of our friendship finally over. But still I am surprised by how calm I feel, how tethered and at peace.

"How are you?" I ask. *"Really?"*

"Fine," he says. "Or as good as can be expected. I have to tell you," he says, "I'm so grateful for our letters. I look forward to every one you send."

"I'm glad to hear that," I say, nodding. "They mean a lot to me, as well."

"They mean the *world* to me," he says, locking his eyes across our empty game board. "It means the world to me that you still write."

"Others must, too," I say, though I know I am the only one. During the first week of his incarceration, Kevin told me once, he received thirty letters—most out of concern, though many of rage—and then the second month only ten, and now there's only ever mine.

People get busy, he wrote. *I'm sure they'll find time to reply soon.*

"It's no problem," I tell him now. "I like that we're still in touch."

For a moment, it is easy to forget that Kevin and I are not in a restaurant, not in a bar, not in a Panera Bread beside a mall. We walk to the row of vending machines and I buy him a pepper and onion pizza in an off-white cardboard box.

"I've been fasting since yesterday," he says. "I've been so excited for this food." The pizza is disgusting—simple marinara over Texas toast—but still Kevin eats it happily, smiling, wiping at his mouth.

"You should get something, too," he says, suddenly self-conscious, but I can't bring myself to do it. I can buy Twizzlers here or elsewhere, at a crappy gas station, at the hotel. Kevin hasn't had Twizzlers in over thirty months.

"Here," I say, sliding the quarters into the machine, and after the Twizzlers release, I eat one slowly in the time it takes him to eat the rest. "I'm full," I say, "I swear."

As our hour draws to a close, Kevin encourages me to stay another. "That's the beauty of being *here*," he says. "I can have guests until three o'clock."

"How about this," I tell him simply. "How about I stay a half hour longer?"

"Sure," he says, nodding. "But if you want, you should stay later." He leans in a little closer until I can smell the scent of his shampoo, see his eyes in perfect bloom. "You know," he says. "Those were the best days of my life. In Gettysburg, I mean."

But I cannot—even out of kindness—repeat that phrase to him.

"Good," I say. I look around at the rows of people reconnecting. "What will you do," I ask, "after I leave and you go back to your cell?"

"I don't know," he says. He pats his pocket, fumbling for

money that is not there. "I have some ideas," he says. "There are things I'm very excited about. I'm going to save up for a typewriter, I think, definitely enroll in classes. I'm beginning to feel some hope, I guess."

Already he has made friends with another man, he tells me, who also reads the *New Yorker*.

"When the new issues come," he says, "they call our names, and we get them at this desk. I was the only one getting them for so long, but the other day someone else showed up."

"Oh?" I ask.

"We've already petitioned to be cell mates," he continues. "I think we'll have a lot in common. I'm writing now, mostly stories. I'm hoping we can share our work, talk about ideas while our minds are fresh."

No longer will he be victim to his mind; he's found a way to make it work for him.

"Maybe after you leave," he says, "I can send you some of my stories? My mom will type them, and maybe you can share your thoughts?"

And *sure*, I say, *of course*, though within six months, I will no longer want to. Within ten, we will no longer be writing each other. The stories and their violence. The female protagonist, murdering a man so violently, the exact specifics of the death so similar to those inflicted upon Emily. My own writing, which he'll later call a betrayal, even after encouraging me to explore my thoughts with language.

"Write anything you want," he told me once. "My permission is the best that I can offer."

That day in his prison, Kevin says only, "The future finally feels bright." He says, "My time is going . . . It is going." He says, "I'm going to take classes, study religion, study philosophy, write a novel. It's going to have a male protagonist. It's going to be a good use of time. I'm going to right the things I can and think often about the things I can't. It has taken me so long," he says finally, "to get to where I am."

And he wants to remember himself in this moment, how I am sitting here beside him, so with our eight remaining quarters, he suggests we try the photo booth. This is something he wrote about in his letter: that a photo would mean so much. *I can't keep the film copy*, he wrote, *but you could scan it and print it on paper. If you mail it to me, I'll tape it to my wall.*

The idea of the photo booth was, of course, alarming: the idea of sitting on his lap. The idea of that tiny, curtained space. As a child, I'd often sat in photo booths inside movie theaters and skating rinks, my friends and I widening our eyes, pulling apart our cheeks to show tongues blue or green from Pixy Stix dust. To sit across from Kevin at a table—sharing conversation and a board game—had seemed to me one thing, but to squeeze inside a photo booth, I was afraid, would force that uneasy reminder: that he is my friend but also a murderer, that he stabbed Emily Silverstein twenty-seven times in the neck and upper torso, and it doesn't matter that he then phoned the police.

It doesn't matter what the psychiatrists deemed the cause.

It cannot matter the guilt he feels, the ownership he took, the sentence he's now serving. The apologetic speech he gave at his sentencing. The apologetic letter he wrote to her family.

"I wish I could take it back every single day," he read.

"I lost control, somehow, but I wish to God it was my life I took."

Three years after the murder and a thousand miles away, I can sit on my couch and forget what he did, if not my proximity to it. I can read his letter and I can forget what first happened. I can trust the authorities that somehow something *did* happen, that something in our body can short-circuit and burst, a wire red and sparking in the drywall of our minds.

I can get over the strangeness of what it is to be Visitor #3, just after his mother and father, and because he's allowed to list ten, there are seven more behind us—Tiffany and Eric and Sam, Andrew, Keith, Thomas, and Brandon—names Kevin put down "just in case," because gaining clearance to be on his visitors list can take months, *so I should do it now*, he wrote, *just in case they ever come*. And what I know that Kevin doesn't is that they won't ever visit—"It's a shame he didn't get the chair," one said the day after Kevin's sentencing, "for the things he did to that young woman"—but for four years, Kevin was our friend. And what does friendship mean if when he needs us most, we're gone?

So I can be here, in this prison. But in a photo booth, there'll no pretending. I'll be sitting on the lap of a murderer. It would be obvious even to me. We would be so close that he could hurt me. I want to think that it would never happen, but who can say?

"We only get one photo," Kevin says to me now, and when I finally bring myself to look at the machine, my mind going over the words I'll use to carefully turn down his offer, I realize there is no booth or curtain or small, intimate space. That it is just a boxy piece of equipment. That the background is empty: a sterile, white cinder-block wall.

"Oh," I say, "sure," and I stand beside him as he scrolls through photos that will serve as our digital backdrop. There's the Eiffel Tower, an underwater scene. We can be on a roller coaster or in a rain forest or deep in space.

We can even be on Everest.

Finally, Kevin selects NO BACKGROUND, and we see our image on the small glass screen.

"You're going to have to make me laugh," he says. He says it quietly, self-consciously, and I try to think of a joke quick but can't. The screen counts down until the flash—3, 2, 1— before finally I think of a joke a boy told me once in Iowa. I was driving him home from a bowling alley, and he was eating a Laffy Taffy, and because he was learning how to read, I asked him to read the wrapper's joke to me out loud.

"What kind of dog has no ears?" I begin to say to Kevin, ready for the emphasized "*Corn* dog!" but I only get to "has" before the flash lights up and breaks.

In the photo that prints at the front desk, my mouth will be open, and my eyes shut.

Epilogue

THIS IS THE ENDING that I wanted, the ending I thought Kevin and I deserved: the car rattling back down the old dirt road, the prison retreating into my rearview, the song on the radio reminding me it is better to have loved and lost. There is an apt metaphor in the horizon, dotted and alive with blue-green hills, and in the house that I finally return to, my mother asking that I please wipe my shoes.

There is meaning, I think, in the flag, oversized and waving above the prison.

There is meaning, I think, in his assessment: that it takes a long time before we feel better.

If the story were mine to write, that visit would conclude—and sweetly—our narrative. The child sitting Indian-style across my chest would hush, fulfilled and asleep in eternal contentment. There would be no anxiety, crushing down. There would be no fear I couldn't shake. I would be the hero, flawless in my compassion. That photo of the two of us—I'd have pinned it above my desk the way I'd once pinned those childhood letters, postmarked from Columbine, Colorado. It would be proof of my engagement, a testament to how much I cared, the evidence so convincing—his big arm slung around my shoulders.

But there are stories, and then there's life. And when I finally confronted the state of my own—sitting across from Kevin, finally, in his maximum-security prison—the physicality of our visit only ushered in a more painful truth: that I had failed him, and repeatedly, at varying degrees over many years. For while I'd sent Kevin countless compassionate letters, always happy to lend an ear and absorb whatever was offered, I'd only ever been brave from a careful distance, the space allotted to me on the page. I'd wanted to visit Kevin for selfish reasons: to allow the grip of my fear to loosen, to prove I was more than a voice echoing, ghostlike, off a page. But in truth, seeing him—his skin and hair and eyes, his body as human, of course, as anyone's—only forced that uneasy reminder that he was not a character I could control, not a mind I'd ever know, and that—in the face of that or any other danger—my natural instinct was still to hide.

For what I'd failed to do in that prison—and in Gettysburg, and in every letter—was give him the very thing I wanted so desperately for myself: bald, unwavering honesty. How else could I advocate the importance of eliminating the negative stigmas surrounding mental illness, encouraging effective and long-lasting treatment, if I was too afraid to admit its presence within my daily life? I'd failed Kevin, and myself, many times this way before, most notably in that upstairs attic, the bayonet leaning against the corner the same way my father's gun always had. My words should never have been *Dr. Dog is indeed very good*, but instead *I know what it's like to want to end your life*.

Visiting Kevin had not caused a smoothing, as I'd hoped, but an affirming of that deeper fear—acknowledgment that my pain was insubstantial in the presence of cowardice, for no amount of grief or needless, incessant yearning would ever make the truth any more bearable, or provide Kevin the help he needed, or salvage Emily from the dead and raise her up to the land of the living. It would never heal the wounds of her friends or family or silence the psychic ringing we all felt and heard.

I'd spent years waiting for Kevin to deposit some sense of closure I felt was necessary to move on, but in truth, that was a gift I had to give myself, and I did so in the months that followed, first in small ways and then monumental, penning what would ultimately prove my final and most sincere, straightforward letter.

I need to clear the air that's fogged between us, I wrote. *I need to tell you everything*.

But it was a moment that did not come easily, and most especially did not come the way I thought it might. It came not through internal processing or revisiting his letters or any textbook or highlighted passage, but instead during a family visit the following month, December, when I again returned to Pennsylvania to stand beside my brother as he prepared his home for his first child. It was nearly Christmas then, and I stood beside him on his porch overlooking a dulled

Pennsylvania cornfield, a small playground, a set of darkening woods. Two and a half years my senior, my brother was the only one in our family still living in Pennsylvania—our parents and younger brother had moved away over the years—and the house where he and his wife now lived was just ten miles from where we'd been raised. Later, after dinner, he led me through his garage to his pickup in the driveway, where he lowered the gate to the truck's bed.

"Look," he said. Inside was a box bigger than my body—a bouncing swing, it played classical music and prerecorded rhythms on a loop. On the cover of the box, the child hung limp over the plastic; the vibrations, I read aloud, help to lull a child to sleep.

"Wow," I said. It was all I could think to say.

My brother and his wife were now eight months along with the pregnancy, and the swing made tangible time's constant passing; nine months was just a fraction of the time I'd spent writing Kevin, and yet in that time, a baby had all but formed, and in my distance—physical, emotional—I'd missed those scenes unfolding: my sister-in-law knitting a blanket above her stomach, my brother kneeling along the carpet, the two of them holding the crib's cherry frame while my father hammered the wooden pieces together.

In the driveway, I looked at the cardboard baby, the cardboard father standing, proud, beyond it.

"Are you scared?" I asked, for surely it's the question my brother most expected; I was two years younger than him but a world behind.

"Yes," he said. A baby was the most fragile thing on earth,

he reminded me, and to have one of his own—whose genetic makeup was half his, whose survival was dependent upon his very own—made it an even more fragile entity. He'd sold his motorcycle, he said, the helmet, the custom riding suit he'd once had made. He'd tailored back his drinking. He'd started a college fund in her name.

He popped the truck gate back into place. "Nothing scares me so much," he said, "but I think that's how you know it's right."

That very evening, in his darkened guest room, I penned a mental note to Kevin confessing everything: my obsession, my former self, the hundred dollars I'd spent on photocopies I'd first ignored and then fanned out, their data and grayscale charts stacked in careful piles across my desk. Addressing Kevin—and myself, of course, by proxy—was the last step afforded to me, but it was also the most important, far beyond any prison visit, any photocopied papers or voyeuristic reading, because it meant addressing reality. We'd long kept secrets from each other, Kevin and I, stowed away our respective private pains, but I wanted—before I lost my chance—to say something worth saying.

Honesty was important, the piece we'd been missing all along, and yet when finally I put those words to paper, I wrote all the while knowing it would prove a fatal breach within our friendship; in expelling what I'd long held inside, I was undoubtedly upsetting the things he was holding, as well. He wanted, desperately, to forget: about Emily, about suicide, about depression—occupy his days, instead, with basketball and word games—and what obligation did he have, in any case, to open up to me about anything? But in offering Kevin full disclosure, I hoped he'd offer me the same, for surely it's what we both wanted—what a relief we'd find in truth. And if he chose not to respond, perhaps that too would be a relief, for however hard it was to receive his letters, it was harder still to pretend their superficiality was not upsetting, that there were not more pressing matters at hand, that his meditations on books and movies were enough to pacify—forever—my haunted mind.

Above all, I wrote, *I hope you know that I feel what happened to you* happened *to you, and I hope that you write back. I want to have this conversation.*

Then, like every decision I've ever made, I threw my whole weight behind it, placing every letter and careful document in a milk crate beside my desk. I liked their efficient placement: how, should he elect not to respond, I could put them in my closet, behind my snow jacket and hats and boots. Behind my vacuum and humidifier and the air conditioner I never used.

How else can I describe the hours and days and weeks that followed? Endless, and eternal. Each morning, I waited for the mailman's jeep to lumber lazily up the road, the anticipation within those moments as great as it had been those first few weeks: I was always waiting, waiting, waiting, if not physically then psychically. Outside, I'd sift through piles of envelopes in the blistering cold, in the freezing rain, in spring's first light, until the truth became all but obvious: It wasn't only I who wanted, desperately, to forget Kevin and Gettysburg. That although I'd never imagined it, Kevin wanted to forget us, too.

. . .

In his often quoted essay "Experience," Ralph Waldo Emerson asserts that human beings are "ghostlike," creatures so desperate to discover an authentic reality that they create their own misery.

The dream world we live in, he writes, is full of illusions, and in our attempts to find reality and experience something true and real, we create suffering. In remarking upon the death of his own son, an experience Emerson felt confident would leave him scarred, he writes it was a more arduous and taxing task to accept the insignificance of his pain—the absolute and brutal futility of how little it amounted to.

"I grieve," he wrote, famously, "that grief can teach me nothing, nor carry me one step into real nature."

This was my mistake, as well, for while I realize now that perhaps it's possible to construct a narrative about Kevin's life—one event that instigated a chain that eventually led him to that April evening, the night shining in puddles on the shallow sidewalk, Emily breaking them in rain boots, approaching the house where she would die—I would be constructing it for the wrong reasons; I'd be constructing it for causation. What I've wanted most, I realized, was never so much an answer about that night, specifically, but to understand the causation behind the thousands of incidents just like it—to know whose responsibility it is, exactly, to ensure the mental health of our nation's men, of our nation's women, teenagers, children. I want to believe that my words would not have changed a thing, and in all likelihood, perhaps they wouldn't have. We can't move backward through time and space, offer aid where we've failed to give it. The truth is, life happens the way it happens, and it's impossible now to know if there even was a chain, or if so, when it began: if Kevin was five, or nine, or twelve, or twenty-one, or twenty-two. Maybe it didn't happen until it happened, that stress stagnating inside his brain, and the truth—what I *believe* is the truth—is that I don't think that Kevin knows, either.

And—regardless of any narrative—Emily is always dead, and Kevin is always the one that killed her.

This is not to say, of course, that I don't still see what happened in everything. This is how trauma works: It manifests in the everyday, in large ways and in small. You can distance yourself from an event, but not the triggers that can reengage it, and it seems—for whatever reason—they often find me in the strangest ways.

On my way to work, for example, I pass an intersection where I have the right-of-way; the people on the intersecting road must stop, and every day, they do. It is a rural road: few passing cars, no streetlights, and it is not particularly demanding of my absolute concentration, so I often take the time to look at the landscape—which, when snowy, is white and endless, not a single tree or rock to interrupt that canvas—or else I fiddle with the radio, try to navigate to something soothing.

Some days, if I'm returning home at dusk, I drive down the center of the road, as my father told me once to do, if not because of the ice along its edges, then the deer that live here in great abundance. The road is flat and fairly straight; I can always see whatever's coming. But one afternoon, as I reached the intersection, a school bus on the adjacent road didn't stop. The driver almost T-boned me. He was going fifty, sixty miles an hour, and I was going just as fast. Surely he knew the stop sign was there—I assume he drove that route daily—but for whatever reason, he didn't recognize it, or his mind didn't send the signal. There was no pause evident in his movement, no urge for his foot to brake, to *stop*. Had I not seen him in the corner of my vision—not rolling but *barreling* through the sign—he would have undoubtedly hit me. And the injuries I would've sustained—it's hard to say how bad or if I'd have survived them in the first place.

Our timing was so exact that if I hadn't slammed on the brakes at the exact moment I did, or had my car been a different shape, a different size, a different model, perhaps the brakes not newly installed, I would have arrived at that particular patch of asphalt at precisely the same time that his bus did.

But the point is: I stopped. Those brakes—because new—had worked. I threw my hands up, slammed the wheel, screamed although I knew he couldn't hear me. He threw his hands up, too, a clear and indisputable apology.

I didn't see you, his look said plainly. *I realize—believe me, I do—just how bad this could have been.*

And for weeks, this thought controlled me: how, in many ways, Emily was at an intersection. She was at an intersection she visited regularly, except this time everything was different. Kevin was supposed to stop—of course he *knew* he had to—but for whatever reason, he did not. And what scares me most of all was, What could Emily, or anyone, do?

I see it in other ways. In the summer of 2013, for example, I rented a farmhouse in the countryside, deeming it a sensible thing to do; I thought the quiet would be of value. The house was beautiful—a hundred years old, but well maintained, with sloping, elegant shutters and a quiet den—and I spent my days beside an apple tree, a blue plank porch, and a hundred acres. It was an old house, cheap, in the middle of absolutely nowhere, and it was for this reason that I'd rented it: I thought it would be useful to be far away. It was August, and the house sat neatly on a hill, the highest point visible for miles.

Those first few weeks, a friend stayed with me—another writer whose work I loved and whose company I adored above all else. We were both single and had been friends for years and agreed it would be nice to split the house while taking solace in each other's company. We were both lost in a figurative sense, the way you are when you are young, the way I think you cannot help but be. Each evening, after our separate days of quiet work, we'd meet on the porch for beer, which we drank straight from aluminum cans. We fanned ourselves with sweaty palms and cooked chicken over hot charcoal and, later, watched the moon from the old plank porch, listening to cattle graze in the field beyond. They made a primitive huffing sound—a demonic sort of snorting—and because we couldn't see them in the darkness from our place along the porch, we had to trust that they were there—that it was cows and not something else.

"The devil's in these woods," my friend would joke, refer-encing her evangelical upbringing, and at night when we brushed our teeth, she'd make guttural sounds in the empty hallway, thinking that this was funny.

But they are cows, I thought, *not demons.*

Life felt easier while she was there. During the day, her sounds kept me company, even while she worked several rooms away. I'd hear the shuffling of her papers, or a chair sliding as she slipped out. But when she left, the house was empty, and at night the rooms grew dark. The cows' sounds traveled across the yard and she was not there to sit beside me.

Don't be afraid, I told myself, because I'd begun working hard at that. *It's only cows*, I told myself. *Just all this land and a bunch of cows.*

There was no demon in those woods.

There was no demon in that house.

But still I felt that fear, because it comes back from time to time. I see my face in a passing mirror, the reflection distorted and dim from the bright, green moonlight, the shadows piling around my eyes, and I feel that dread, like I fear I always will. For a second, that face registers and looks nothing like my own. It looks like someone else's face entirely. I lean in closer to examine it, the way I did when I was six, my friends and I daring each other in bathrooms to hold our gaze in the vanity, saying, "Bloody Mary, Bloody Mary," until our features became unfamiliar, until we felt like ghosts ourselves.

It's that reflection—that foreign feeling—that proves what I trust, somehow, to be true: how what I've identified in Kevin is something I'm nearly certain is in everyone.

. . .

So it is not a distant pinpoint; I do not feel as though I'm on a shore. Still, the worst of it is over, and for that, I think, I'm glad. My friend—a scientist—reminds me that human beings are resilient; when given the opportunity, he explains, our bodies will always move toward health. The mind will move, too, in ways, deleting its memories as it sees fit. Kevin frightens me, I think, not because of who he is or even what he's done but because of how similar we are, indeed how similar we all are, how the chain of events that led to Emily's death are events that could happen to any of us.

And yet I am all too aware of the way that grief can overwrite a person. Upon completion of *In Cold Blood*, for example, Truman Capote allegedly found himself so racked by grief and sorrow he never again completed a full-length work. And in the epigraph he chose for his uncompleted novel, he wrote, *More tears are shed over answered prayers than unanswered ones*, which is a grief I think I understand.

So when I think about my life now, I find I think, often, about bugs. What I mean, here, are the insects that swirl around a porch light and pool in clusters above the doorframe. That summer in that farmhouse—they bobbed beneath the bulb, spinning themselves in dizzy circles, and from my place just underneath them, I found myself thinking, *I am just like them*.

I became fascinated with their movement. I realized: *Those bugs can't get away.*

If you'd asked me weeks, or months, or even years before that night, I wouldn't be able to tell you why bugs are so attracted to light. They just are; it's not an especially new or interesting phenomenon. But now I know—because I've looked it up—that bugs function with an inefficient navigational system; evolution gave them a way to move only by the light of the moon, and so they buzz in relation to its location. It is the only way they know where they are or are trying to go. Our artificial lights—which blink and bing and buzz— create a chaos that throws them off. And because they can't navigate our world, they instead become literally *incapable* of independent movement, likely believing that they are leaving when in reality they're only circling, flying around in dumb, tight patterns, horribly ineffective loops.

And sometimes, in the quietest moments, I think that murder made me like those broken bugs. It follows me everywhere, across many states, many stages of living. I am the bug that can't escape.

I blink and buzz but spin.

Still, it seems to me there's a choice: We can navigate the best we can with whatever system we've been given, or we can fly around aimlessly, become complicit in our own failure. With bugs, the light eventually shuts off, or the light eventually runs dry. But the energy of a trauma only reignites itself again and again.

The trick, I think, is this: You have to disengage it. Remember it was the moon that once famously led you there, and trust with all your being that the moon can also lead you away.

The last I heard of Kevin, he had finally enrolled in classes.

He was planning an advanced degree and asked a former friend to tell me not to write him. That same month, I was offered a job just three hours away from Albion, so while I am now the closest I have ever been, I have also never been so far.

The change, I think, is healthy. I think about my brother, the bravery it takes to have a child: what it is to bring something into this world despite the obstacles you don't know to fear. That December night, after supper, I followed him through their kitchen and down the hall to where his wife sat reading, and I watched as he bent down, placing his hand along her sweater.

"Health of body," Emerson writes, "consists in circulation." When we dedicate ourselves to only one idea or concept—one fear, as was my case—we do so in utter error. In permanence, he writes, we find death, but in change, we can find life.

The light was low as my brother bent down, as he gestured to me with his hand, and when he took my palm in his and placed it lightly along the fabric, I felt—for the first time— what love and fear somehow made kick.

Acknowledgments

This book would not exist without the careful consideration, mentorship, and support of so many people to whom I wish to extend my utmost gratitude. Thanks especially to the University of Iowa's Nonfiction Writing Program and Colgate University for giving me the time and financial means to write this book, to say nothing of the tremendous guidance, support, and encouragement offered by their administrations and faculties.

I've been blessed to have many terrific teachers and mentors over the years—most especially, thank you to Robin Hemley, who believed in this project from the beginning, as well as John D'Agata, whose guidance has proved invaluable. Thank you, too, to David Hamilton, Patricia Foster, and Bonnie Sunstein, and a special thanks, as well, to Meghan Daum, who offered insight on this book's earliest iteration. I'm also deeply grateful to my brilliant and warm former colleagues in the Department of English at Colgate University, especially Jennifer Brice, Peter Balakian, Jane Pinchin, and Tess Jones.

A special thank you, as well, to Gregory Ames and Chinelo Okparanta for their friendship and company in the midst of the hardest chapters.

I've had the honor of working with many amazing, patient editors over the years, and I'm especially grateful to the editors of journals in which portions of this book first appeared: "Sick" in *The Rumpus*, "Light Up and Break" in *The Colorado Review*, "Lessons of Grief" in *Vela*, "My Friend, the Murderer" in *Salon*, "Why It's Called a Life Sentence" in *Guernica*, and "Reenacting" in *The Iowa Review*. In particular, thanks to editors Stephanie G'Schwind, Molly Beer, Lynne Nugent, Aditi Sriram, Simone Gorrindo, Elissa Bassist, Aaron Burch, Daniel Torday, Tom McAllister, Dave Housley, and Mike Ingram. A final and heartfelt thanks to guest judge David Shields for awarding an excerpt of this book, "Reenacting," the 2014 Iowa Review Award in nonfiction.

My deepest thanks to agent and friend, Samantha Shea, for her early support of my manuscript and for believing in its potential when I wasn't entirely sure I did, and a deep thank you, as well, to her terrific team at Georges Borchardt, Inc. I am lucky to have an incredible editor in Vanessa Kehren, tireless and fearsome champion of words, and I am genuinely blessed to have found a home for this book with Blue Rider Press.

Thank you to John Casteen, who is brilliant beyond words, as well as Mary Miller and David Torrey Peters, both first readers, whose early support and feedback proved invaluable.

There are so many people whose friendship and compassion shaped this book in various ways. Thank you especially to Dylan Nice and Rachel Yoder, both talented beyond measure, writers whose love of words I've long found contagious. A special thanks also to Alyssa Starman, Caleb Baker, Seth Michel, Cutter Wood, Erin Shaw, Mieke Eerkens, Tim Denevi, Jennifer Percy, Kristen Radtke, Kerry Howley, Will Wilkinson, Kendra Greene, Annie Nilsson, Nina Feng, Aaron Burch, Elizabeth Ellen, Kristen Forbes, Eliza Smith, Amanda Goldblatt, Chloe Caldwell, Leslie Jamison, Jill Talbot, Marisa Trettel, Kellen Thomas, Kevin Metz, Kenneth Nace, Caryn Cardello, Marilyn Abildskov, Kelly Sundberg, Stephen Lovely, Roger Schmidt, Jessica Krichels, Cherie Hacker, Tracy Turner, Javier Barboza, Geoff Calver, Tara Irwin, and Ben Leddick.

Thanks to the staffs of Adams County Courthouse and the Albion State Correctional Institution, who dutifully and promptly provided insight, and to select members of the Gettysburg College community who helped corroborate key details or otherwise supported me during this endeavor.

To my family—the most heartfelt *thank you* for supporting my crazy dream and helping make that dream a reality. In particular, thank you to my parents, Heidi and John, to whom this book is dedicated with my absolute admiration and love.

The sincerest thanks to Kevin Schaeffer, and for his friendship for as long as it lasted.

Finally, thank you to the communities of Iowa City, Iowa; Hamilton, New York; and Washington, New Hampshire— the most idyllic landscapes within which to write a book, and my beloved homes these past many years.

Bibliography

"Antidepressant Medications for Children and Adolescents: Information for Parents and Caregivers." National Institute of Mental Health. http://www.nimh.nih.gov/health/topics/child-and-adolescent-mental-health/antidepressant-medications-for-children-and-adolescents-information-for-parents-and-caregivers.shtml.

Breggin, Peter R. "The Proven Dangers of Antidepressants." Psychiatric Drug Facts with Dr. Peter Breggin. http://www.breggin.com/. Consulted November 12, 2013.

Busey, John W., and David G. Martin. *Regimental Strengths and Losses at Gettysburg*. Hightstown, NJ: Longstreet House, 1994.

Cobb, Chris. "Gruesome Case Videos Became Too Much for Top Psychiatrist Trained to Analyze Twisted Minds of Sexual Sadists." *National Post* (Canada), November 11, 2013. http://news.nationalpost.com/2013/11/11/how-the-go-to-guy-for-lawyers-needing-to-understand-the-twisted-minds-of-sexual-sadists-descended-into-ptsd/.

Epstein, Mark. "The Trauma of Being Alive." *The New York Times*, August 3, 2013. http://www.nytimes.com/2013/08/04/opinion/sunday/the-trauma-of-being-alive.html?pagewanted=all&_r=0.

Follman, Mark, Gavin Aronsen, and Deanna Pan. "A Guide to Mass Shootings in America." *Mother Jones*, February 27, 2013, updated May 24,

2014. http://www.motherjones.com/politics/2012/07/mass-shootings -map.

Gorman, James. "Scientists Trace Memories of Things That Never Happened." *The New York Times*, July 25, 2013. http://www.nytimes.com /2013/07/26/science/false-memory-planted-in-a-mouse-brain-study -shows.html.

Gray, Katti. "The Run-On Sentence: Eddie Ellis on Life After Prison." *The Sun Magazine*, July 2013. http://thesunmagazine.org/issues/451/the_run _on_sentence.

Green, Amanda. "The Rumpus Interview with Sabine Heinlein." *The Rumpus*, October 17, 2013. http://therumpus.net/2013/10/the-rumpus-inter view-with-sabine-heinlein/.

Gunderman, Richard. "The Incarceration Epidemic." *The Atlantic*, June 20, 2013. http://www.theatlantic.com/health/archive/2013/06/the-incarcera tion-epidemic/277056/.

Hardesty, Katherine, Ph.D., and Judith E. Sturges, Ph.D., with the collaboration of the Pennsylvania Department of Corrections. *A Handbook for the Families and Friends of Pennsylvania Department of Corrections.* Revised and updated by Pennsylvania Department of Corrections personnel. Pennsylvania Department of Corrections, November 2006. https://www.google .com/search?q=A+Handbook+for+the+Families+and+Friends+of+Penn sylvania+Department+of+Corrections&ie=utf-8&oe=utf-8&aq=t&rls =org.mozilla:it:official&client=firefox-a&channel=sb.

"Harper's Index." *Harper's Magazine*, August and November 2013. http:// harpers.org/archive/2013/08/harpers-index-352/ and http://harpers.org /archive/2013/11/harpers-index-355/.

Ho, Dien, Ph.D. "Antidepressants and the FDA's Black-Box Warning: Determining a Rational Public Policy in the Absence of Sufficient Evidence." *Virtual Mentor* 14, no. 6 (June 1, 2012), 483–488. http://virtualmentor .ama-assn.org/2012/06/pfor2-1206.html.

"Interview: Robert Bly." *No Safe Place: Violence Against Women*. PBS, March 27, 1998. http://www.pbs.org/kued/nosafeplace/interv/bly.html.

Jenkins, Mark. "Gettysburg: From Battlefield to Civil War Shrine." *National Geographic*, July 14, 2003. http://news.nationalgeographic.com/news/2003 /07/0714_030714_gettysburg.html.

Kimmel, Michael. "Masculinity, Mental Illness and Guns: A Lethal Equation?" CNN: Living, December 19, 2012. http://www.cnn.com/2012/12 /19/liv-ing/men-guns-violence/.

Klebold, Susan. "I Will Never Know Why." *O, the Oprah Magazine*, November 2009. http://www.oprah.com/world/Susan-Klebolds-O-Magazine -Essay-I-Will-Never-Know-Why.

Long, Liza. "'I Am Adam Lanza's Mother': A Mom's Perspective on the Mental Illness Conversation in America." *The Huffington Post*, December 16, 2012, updated May 13, 2014. http://www.huffingtonpost.com/2012/12 /16/i-am-adam-lanzas-mother-mental-illness-conversation_n_2311009 .html.

Murphy, Meghan. "What Is It About Men That They're Committing These Horrible Massacres?" AlterNet, December 18, 2012. http://www.alternet .org/gender/what-it-about-men-theyre-committing-these-horrible -massacres.

Nesbitt, Mark. *Ghosts of Gettysburg: Spirits, Apparitions and Haunted Places of the Battlefield*. Gettysburg, PA: Thomas Publications, 1991.

Orange, Michelle. "The Uses of Nostalgia and Some Thoughts on Ethan Hawke's Face." In *This Is Running for Your Life: Essays*. New York: Farrar, Straus and Giroux, 2013.

Power, Matthew. "Confessions of a Drone Warrior." *GQ*, October 23, 2013. http://www.gq.com/news-politics/big-issues/201311/drone-uav-pilot -assassination.

Raison, Charles. "Psychiatrist: I Hate Suicide But Also Understand It." CNN: Health, August 21, 2012. http://www.cnn.com/2012/08/21/health/ raison-suicide-tony-scott/.

Sacks, Oliver. "Speak, Memory." *The New York Review of Books*, February 21, 2013. http://www.nybooks.com/articles/archives/2013/feb/21/speak -memory/.

Sears, Stephen W. *Gettysburg*. Boston: Houghton Mifflin, 2003.

Szalavitz, Maia. "Top Ten Legal Drugs Linked to Violence." *Time*: Body & Mind, January 7, 2011. http://healthland.time.com/2011/01/07/top-ten -legal-drugs-linked-to-violence/.

"25 Deadliest Mass Shootings in U.S. History Fast Facts." CNN: U.S., September 2, 2014. http://www.cnn.com/2013/09/16/us/20-deadliest-mass -shootings-in-u-s-history-fast-facts/.

"Unemployment Rates for States." United States Department of Labor, Bureau of Labor Statistics, 2009. http://www.bls.gov/lau/lastrk09.htm.

White, Ronald C., Jr. *The Eloquent President: A Portrait of Lincoln Through His Words*. New York: Random House, 2005.

About the Author

Amy Butcher's work has appeared in *The New York Times*, *The New York Times Magazine*, *The Paris Review* online, *Tin House* online, *The Iowa Review*, *Salon*, *Gulf Coast*, *Guernica*, and *Brevity*, among others. She earned her MFA from the University of Iowa and is the recipient of awards and grants from the Kimmel Harding Nelson Center for the Arts, the Stanley Foundation for International Research, the Academy of American Poets, and Colgate University's Olive B. O'Connor Creative Writing Fellowship. The winner of the 2014 Iowa Review Award in nonfiction, Butcher teaches writing at Ohio Wesleyan University.